which?
essential guides

WORKING
FOR YOURSELF

66 Do you dream of running your own business?
To succeed you need to plan, research, and take
advice. Most important of all you need to give it
everything you've got. 99

Mike Pywell and Bill Hilton

About the authors

Mike Pywell has experience in all areas of business life:
as an employee, a corporate executive, a self-employed
entrepreneur and an adviser to small businesses. He has
spent the last two years working with Avanta Enterprises Ltd
to develop and launch www.businessclub365.com, a support
site for business start-ups and established small businesses.

Bill Hilton is a writer and corporate communications
specialist with a particular interest in copywriting and
blogging. He has considerable experience of writing for
business and providing strategic advice on web marketing,
product blogs and internet trends.

which?
essential guides

WORKING
FOR YOURSELF

Mike Pywell and Bill Hilton

Which? Books are commissioned and published by Which? Ltd,
2 Marylebone Road, London NW1 4DF
Head of Which? Books: Angela Newton
Project management for Which? Books: Luke Block
Email: books@which.co.uk

Distributed by Littlehampton Book Services Ltd, Faraday Close, Durrington, Worthing,
West Sussex BN13 3RB

British Library Cataloguing in Publication Data
A catalogue record for this book is available from the British Library

Authors' acknowledgments
The authors would like to thank their families for their support, Clive Lawrence-Forbes
for reading the drafts and offering useful insights, and the teams at InBiz and
BusinessClub365.com for their passion and commitment to self-employment.

Edited and additional text by: Victoria Walker
Designed by: Philip Jansseune and Gillian Healey for Walker Jansseune
Index by: Lynda Swindells
Cover photographs by: Mark Wood, Alamy Images
Printed and bound by Scotprint, Scotland

For a full list of Which? Books, please call 01903 828557, access our website at
www.which.co.uk, or write to Littlehampton Book Services.
For other enquiries call 0800 252 100.

Contents

Introduction

If you are thinking of leaving your job to become self-employed, this book is for you. Our focus is on becoming a one man (or woman) band: from getting started and winning business, to managing your time, money, working environment and, crucially, your life.

You will find this book useful if you are thinking of working for yourself in any number of careers, including:

- Plumber, plasterer, builder or electrician.
- Freelance writer, personal assistant or administrator.
- Musician or entertainer.
- Programmer, designer or internet trader.
- Consultant or sales agent.

You do not have to restrict yourself to one role. Many self-employed people have 'portfolio careers' that combine a number of different skills. For example, you might spend most of your time as a bookkeeper, but also do some landscape gardening. You could plaster walls two days a week and run an ecommerce website on the other three.

One of the chief attractions of starting up on your own is the freedom it offers. You are free from your boss, free to set your own hours and free to manage your own destiny.

You are also free to fail, and many do. If you start your own business you are probably a bold and enterprising individual. But boldness and enterprise alone will not see you through. You need

determination, patience and a willingness to plan ahead. You will find that most triumphs, like most disasters, are temporary. You need the dedication to work through both, always learning lessons and building relationships within your marketplace.

You also need good advice. When you start out, it will seem that everyone has something to say about the best way to run your business: your friends and family, your bank, even the government. Unfortunately, as we will see, not all advice is good, and much of it is biased. Our aim is to give you the kind of advice you can rely on. We will use case studies of real self-employed people and learn from their successes and their failures.

YOUR MOTIVATIONS

Before we look at the nuts and bolts of self-employment, it is worth taking a look at yourself and asking: 'Why do I want to leave the security of my job and venture into uncharted territory?'

There are positive and negative reasons for becoming self-employed. Most people who start up in business for themselves usually come to self-employment with a mixture of both.

You might find working nine-to-five dull and repetitive (negative) and also want to have a go at making more money than your employer pays you (positive).

Think hard about your motivations. If they are all negative, take a long, hard look at yourself. Are your feelings about your current job negative for reasons that are out of your control, or because you tend to take a pessimistic, downbeat view of life? If it is the latter, perhaps you should be wary of self-employment. Taking responsibility for your own income, forming relationships with clients and winning business need a positive, 'can-do' attitude. It is good to be sceptical, but a negative attitude is a big handicap in business, and lack of self-belief is a major reason for small business failure.

On the other hand, you should not become self-employed if you think it is an easy life and a great way of getting rich quick. Although self-employment is often both financially and emotionally rewarding, your business is unlikely to take off overnight. So before you decide how you are going to run a business, and certainly before you quit your job, you need to decide why you want to do it.

❝ If you start your own business you are probably a bold and enterprising individual. ❞

Timing your jump

Switching from employment to self-employment needs careful planning. If you are starting out unexpectedly, your first months will probably be financially tougher than if you had already made preparations to work for some time without a guaranteed salary. Very few businesses make much profit in their first few months, because it takes time to build a customer base and reputation.

So try not to make the transition too suddenly. On the other hand, do not be too cautious, either. According to the Department for Business, Enterprise and Regulatory Reform, (formerly the Department of Trade and Industry), at any one time approximately two million people are thinking about self-employment, but only 400,000 new businesses are launched every year. In other words, 20 per cent of those who are interested in working for themselves actually take action. Don't fall into the trap of just dreaming about self-employment if you have the skills and determination to actually do it.

However, it is difficult to start a business without risk. Those risks can relate to finance, security, relationships, status, and perhaps most important of all, the risk of failure. You may find yourself hesitating and asking: 'is it wise to risk all I've got, what if it goes wrong?'

The simple answer is that you'll never know if you never start. You need to put fear of failure behind you and concentrate on how to make a success. If you believe it is not going to work, it probably won't. Belief in yourself, almost above everything else, is the most important ingredient for success.

The beauty about today's world is that it is not necessary to risk everything. Many businesses can be launched on a part-time basis, or can even be run virtually, so that you have the opportunity to trial your idea and test your approach before launching for real.

But what about risk? Launching any business will contain an element of risk. Most people who have succeeded in life have taken risks, and it can often be the risks that present make or break situations that ultimately produce the performance that makes the difference.

If you're going to be successful in running your own business, you have to be prepared to give it everything you've got. If you do that, and take good advice along the way, there is every reason why you should succeed. But you still have to take that first step.

Once you are self-employed you will be making decisions every day. The first decision of your business career is whether or not to actually get started. Think about it carefully, then act.

"Belief in yourself, almost above everything else, is the most important ingredient for success."

The small business lifestyle

Starting a business will change your life. You – and your family, if you have one – will make the jump more easily if you consider some of the less obvious effects of self-employment.

1

Ready for business?

As you read this, there is a good chance that you're already earning an income in a full-time or part-time job. Even if you are not, you have probably already given some thought to the differences between employment and being self-employed.

At first, the benefits and disadvantages of self-employment seem obvious. On the upside, you get:

- Freedom to set your own hours and place of work.
- The opportunity to earn more.
- Independence from your boss.
- A chance to fulfil your ambitions.

While the possible downsides include:

- An uncertain income.
- No free employment perks.
- No holiday pay, work pension or basic sick pay.
- The risk of failure.

But some of these advantages and disadvantages are not what they seem. Freedom to set your own hours may sound great when you are stuck in a nine-to-five grind. But if you are a motivated person, deciding when and how you work has its disadvantages; it can be hard to drag yourself away when the jobs are piling up, or you are fighting for business. Overwork is a big problem among the self-employed, and it can lead to health and relationship difficulties if you push yourself too hard.

THE REALITY OF RISK

A popular myth is that working for someone else is more secure than running your own business. That may be true if you are in a career with reasonable long-term prospects, like teaching. But very few jobs have that kind of security these days. Technology and the internet have led many organisations to change the way they work, and those changes are continuing. Tasks are increasingly outsourced to contractors, many of them overseas. In this rapidly-evolving work environment, very few employed workers are in a position to say that their job and promotion prospects are secure for life. What you imagine is a permanent role may, a few years down the line, be given to an outside contractor, or a computer, to perform.

So taking the initiative and becoming self-employed while your career is still on its upswing can actually be a less risky option than staying where you are, especially if you can make your former employer one of your first clients.

THE BEST ADVICE?

When you start thinking about launching your own business, you will probably seek professional advice from a business adviser, bank manager or accountant. They can help you with making the financial transition from employment to self-employment, and you are much more likely to succeed if you listen to them. But do not neglect the real experts; the people who have been there and done it.

These people have not just changed their jobs by becoming self-employed. They have made an emotional and mental change. Talk to people who are already self-employed and benefit from their experience. Ask them to tell you how running a business has altered the way they live their lives, for better and for worse.

THE BIG DIFFERENCES

Starting your own business also means changing the way you work and making your job much more a part of your life. It can be a lot more difficult to draw a line between your home life and your professional life, especially if your head office is in the spare bedroom.

Jack of all trades?

Even if you dream of turning your business into a multinational giant, you are going to be small when you start, so you will not have the luxury of a large staff. You will have to be a jack of all trades: as well as performing your key role you will have to answer the phones, do the administration and look after a hundred other tasks. Crucially, you will have to promote your business. Many perfectly good start-ups fail because their owners don't understand the importance of marketing, or even how to do it. We cover marketing in detail in Chapter 7.

Goodbye boss!

When you're newly self-employed, you may struggle to adjust to not having a boss. With no manager keeping a check on progress, you will need to be completely self-disciplined. You will not be able to pass problems up the line. The buck will stop very firmly with you.

Statements from people who have recently started-up

- 'It can be hard, not having a fixed routine. You have to be self-disciplined to get out of bed in the morning and get the job done.'

- 'My family and friends think that because I work from home I'm always available to do favours and run errands...'

- 'When I was at work, a day used to seem like forever. Now they go too quickly. Time just vanishes!'

- 'Now that I have an irregular income I'm much better at managing my personal finances.'

- 'I'd never go back to working for someone else.'

❝A popular myth is that working for someone else is more secure than running your own business.❞

The problem of credit

As a self-employed entrepreneur you're helping to drive the nation's economy: congratulations. Unfortunately, your bank or building society will perceive you as a risk and your credit rating will probably dip. People in full-time employment are a very safe bet for finance and mortgages, the self-employed are not. Loans and mortgages will be pricier and harder to come by. Unless you self-certificate (which can be expensive), you are unlikely to get a mortgage if you have been trading for fewer than three years.

Never forget, though, that when you become self-employed there's no real limit on your income, as there is when you're working for an employer. You might have to tighten your belt to start with, but one day you might be a millionaire.

Friends and family

Most businesses have to work hard to become established, and even the most supportive partners and families can get jittery. If you hear the words 'go and get a proper job' (and you probably will), console yourself with the knowledge that thousands of entrepreneurs have heard the same words from husbands, wives, partners and parents in the past. If anything, negativity like this should just make you more determined to succeed.

Your friends and colleagues may be more positive, but do not rely on them to stay that way. Many will have considered self-employment and decided against it. They may not want you to succeed at something they were wary of even trying, so do not be surprised if they try to dissuade you. As far as you can, seek advice from people who can view your situation objectively.

Leaving the team

If you already have a job you are probably part of a group of peers that discusses business issues, shares gossip and chats about what was on TV last night. Once you are self-employed you will either be working alone, or you'll be the boss of your own team. You may find you miss the social support a peer group offers.

There are ways of compensating for this. There are plenty of networking clubs, both on the internet and in the real world, that can provide excellent social support. Importantly, they can also be a great source of business!

The drive for results

In a full-time job you can march around the office with a clipboard, looking busy, or call a support centre to order the spare part you can't find. You will still get paid. Being self-employed, having a slack day means earning less money. And there is no back-up team to solve your problems.

The biggest difference between working for somebody else and working for yourself is how you get paid. Work for somebody else and you get paid for

❝ As a self-employed entrepreneur you are helping to drive the nation's economy. ❞

being at work. Work for yourself and you only get paid when you sell your product or service and bank the cheque.

GETTING THE JOB DONE

In self-employment, productivity is everything: you can take a few hours off to see your son play football, or you can meet your partner in town for a coffee. But these pleasures can only be enjoyed if you are productive when you need to be. The most telling changes to your lifestyle will be related to making the transition from rewards based on work to rewards based on results.

Some people fail to make that transition. They think that the self-employed lifestyle is all about flexible working days and charging by the hour. In reality, self-employment is at least as demanding as a paid job. If you are the type of person who can accept responsibility, make difficult decisions, and cope with major changes to the way they live their life, you stand a very good chance of success.

Jargon Buster

Self-certification mortgage Mortgages for the self-employed who cannot produce two or three years' worth of accounts backed by an accountant. These tend to demand payment at a higher rate to minimise risk, although the market is becoming more competitive and deals are improving. You also still have the option to switch to a different lender or a better rate after a few years have elapsed.

Home or office?

Where you work may be dictated by what you decide to do. For example, as a self-employed plumber you'll not have much choice except to work in other people's homes and businesses. But many self-employed people need a base. The question is, do you work out of your home or pay for a separate workspace?

Working from home can be a very attractive and cost-efficient option, particularly if you are doing a job that doesn't need much more than a desk, a telephone and somewhere to plug in your laptop. Even manual or craft-based businesses can be run from home. Artists can set up their easels in a back bedroom, joiners can turn a shed or garage into a workshop and caterers can do everything from the comfort and convenience of their own kitchens. Home working is not only cheap and convenient; you can also write off a proportion of your household bills and expenses against tax.

Taking on outside premises can be expensive and less convenient, but sometimes it is necessary. To understand why, we need first to take a look at some of the disadvantages of working from home.

Managing the work/life balance

Any homeworker will tell you that running a business out of the back bedroom can be cost-effective and provide great flexibility. You do not need to leave keys with the neighbours to let the plumber in.

You are around to collect parcels, so they do not get dragged all the way back to the sorting office. Your lunch break can be spent on the sofa rather than sat on a bench outside the office.

You will soon discover the downsides. Because you are at home, friends and family often don't think you are really working. You will be asked to run errands, and people will call at all times of the day expecting you to be available to chat. Your children will want to know why you cannot drive them around or fix their bikes.

And that is not all: working at home can completely wreck the divide between your work and your home life. If you struggle to motivate yourself you will find it easy to become distracted at home. Daytime TV may become weirdly addictive when you have got work to do and deadlines around the corner. Equally, if you are even remotely obsessive about your work, (and most successful self-employed people are), you will find it difficult to drag yourself away from work at evenings and weekends. This may lead to strained relationships, a diminished social life and increased tiredness.

Having a workspace separate from your home encourages focus. You may even find that the increase in productivity covers the cost of your rent.

Case Study Jacqui

Jacqui is a piano teacher. When she started her business she was well aware of the problems of bringing pupils into her home. As well as thinking about health and safety, she has to comply with child protection regulations. Her business adviser initially suggested that she visited pupils in their houses, using their own pianos or taking an electronic keyboard with her. Jacqui dismissed this idea on professional grounds: she feels it is important that her pupils learn to play on a real, good quality piano. She has to keep her house clean and tidy, and pay out for Public Liability insurance because members of the public are visiting her home. However, her insistence on a first-class learning experience has given her a reputation for integrity and professionalism in her area.

Limitations of space

Depending on the type of self-employment you choose, you may find that your own home simply is not big enough. This may happen if you start a business that grows quickly. If you become the most popular provider of wedding cakes in your area, for example, you'll quickly find that one kitchen work surface and one oven (not to mention one pair of hands), are not enough to fulfil the orders that pour in. Likewise, if you run a successful consultancy or administration business, you may find that all of your filing cabinets and computer equipment take up too much space. Although you have to pay for commercial premises, you may find that if your self-employment grows into a full-blown business operation that perhaps employs other people, you have little choice but to move out of the back bedroom.

Health, safety and insurance

If your business involves people visiting you, working out of your own home can prove to be a legal headache. If you are inviting members of the public on to your property, you need Public Liability insurance to cover against any accidents that may happen to them. You also need to take reasonable steps to maintain their health and safety, which means making sure they are not likely to trip over your children's toys or be savaged by your dog.

In some careers, you might find it difficult to run a public-facing business anywhere else except your home – Jacqui the piano teacher in our case study is a

 The Health and Safety Executive has a number of useful documents outlining health and safety for homeworkers on their website, www.hse.gov.uk

case in point. In a situation like that, you need to make sure you are fully insured and aware of the requirements of health and safety law.

Case Study   Richard

Richard is an independent financial adviser (IFA), offering advice to members of the public on savings, investments and pensions. Although he was initially tempted to work from home, and perhaps visit his clients in their homes, he decided that it was important to have business premises. He wants prospective clients to see him as an honest, reputable, established practitioner in his field. His premises consist of a double office just outside his local town centre, tastefully advertised by a professional-looking brass plate outside the door. He has a double office, allowing him to employ a secretary and have a comfortable waiting area for clients.

The question of image

A final reason you might think again about working from home is tied up with the way your customers perceive you. There is no shame in working from home, but if you are working in a relatively high profile business role, your kitchen table might not be the best place for meetings with clients. You might also consider whether you need a more professional-sounding address than your home offers. A business that operates out of 29 Parkside Avenue may not inspire as much confidence in its customers as one that is based in Enterprise House, Anytown. If you are not planning on having customers visit your home, you can simply register a name change with the Post Office. But if you anticipate entertaining professional visitors on a regular basis, office premises might be more suitable.

If you are planning to work on an international scale, it is also worth knowing that different cultures have different perceptions of single person businesses. In the UK, being a freelance carries a relatively high social status. However, American and (especially) East Asian customers tend to regard self-employed people with some suspicion. Appearing to be bigger than you in fact are can be an advantage in these circumstances, which might mean working out of professional premises with a secretary, or using the services of a telephone answering service.

Case Study   Adam

Adam is a self-employed web designer. He lives by himself, and his two-bedroom flat is ideal for running his business. He has converted one bedroom into an office, but he has also installed a wireless network so he can work anywhere in the flat. However, because he realises the importance of meeting clients face-to-face where possible, he usually has to travel to meet them or find a separate location. He reckons this is a reasonable price to pay for working in the comfort of his own home.

Virtual and roaming offices

Modern technology can free you from traditional ways of working. Using a virtual office enables you to run a complex operation from the comfort of your home, while mobile computing and wireless communications allow you to work more or less anywhere.

If you are going to make the most of the flexibility that technology offers, you have to be aware of its weaknesses as well as its strengths, and start off with a good idea of exactly what can be achieved. If you are intending to run a business on entirely virtual lines, as an eBay trader for example, it is useful to develop some working practices in advance that will help you adjust to this radically new way of working.

VIRTUAL WORKING

The idea behind a virtual office is very simple. Although you are working out of your back bedroom (or on a park bench, or in a pub) you have, through the medium of the internet, access to all the means of doing business that you would have if you were sat in an office surrounded by employees. You can, in theory, live a homeworking lifestyle while running a large, complex business.

At the heart of virtual working lies the idea of outsourcing – subcontracting aspects of your work to other people in remote locations. Working like this can benefit a surprising range of businesses. For example, if you are working as an electrician or a freelance tree surgeon,

there might be times of the day when it is difficult to answer your phone. You do not want to miss out on the chance of new business, but equally it can be quite expensive to hire a full-time secretary to handle calls for you.

Virtual working provides the solution. There are many companies that offer a telephone answering service, fielding calls and forwarding messages to you via voicemail or email. You can go even further and hire a virtual Personal Assistant, a remote worker whom you might never even meet, but who takes your calls and handles your diary. This is cheaper than taking on a full-time PA because the virtual equivalent will look after the needs of half a dozen or more self-employed workers, spreading the cost between you all.

The IT department you never meet

The concept of working virtually can be taken even further. Say you are earning your money by running an ecommerce website. If your business takes off, you may find that you need help from technical specialists. Even if you have programming skills yourself, you probably

Network Support

Bookkeeper

You

PA

IT Support

Marketing

same time zone. Many UK businesses using virtual office systems take advantage of the low prices offered by IT providers in India and other Asian countries.

If you manage it carefully, you can build up the equivalent of quite a large organisation through your virtual office.

Outsourcing via the internet is a great way of getting work done for a good price, but you should double-check the credentials and experience of any provider before you hire them. Many providers offer a bidding service, allowing you to post a project online. Potential providers submit proposals and cost estimates, giving you a detailed shortlist to choose from.

Remember, if you have freelance skills you can also use these providers to sell your services. As well as programming, writing, translation and web design, many major outsourcing websites run marketplaces for marketing consultants, composers, architects and a huge range of other professions.

want to spend your time managing the business rather than tinkering around with online shopping carts. Equally, you may not want the expense of hiring a full-time technical specialist.

Outsourcing solves the problem. You can hire an IT business to do the work for you. Because much of the communication you need to do with your provider can take place via email, you do not need to choose someone who lives nearby, or even in the

Major outsourcing websites

Freelancers Network – UK-based freelance provider for projects and jobs requiring graphic design, programming, copywriting, proofreading, sales and marketing.
www.freelancers.net

Freelancers in the UK – UK-based freelance provider for projects and jobs requiring accountancy, bookkeeping,

payroll, illustration, copywriting, event management, researchers, hairdressing and photography.
www.freelancersintheuk.co.uk

Elance – America-based freelance provider for projects requiring graphic design, programming, copywriting, business support and other services including administration and legal support.
www.elance.com

Guru – America-based freelance provider for projects and jobs requiring creative, IT, business consulting, office and administration skills.
www.guru.com

RentACoder – America-based freelance provider for projects and jobs requiring software coders and developers.
www.rentacoder.com

The Challenges

Your lifestyle will benefit most from virtual working if you are aware of its limitations. The main problems you will come across will be caused by communication or, rather, miscommunication.

That may seem ridiculous. After all, the internet is supposed to have turned the world into a 'global village', where we can just fire up our computers and then talk to more or less anyone. That is true to an extent. But it is also important to remember that in some senses electronic communications are a step backwards. More business is carried out in writing these days than at any time since the nineteenth century. The telephone is used less than it was a decade ago.

The problem with an email message is that it is essentially nothing more than a glorified, high-speed carrier pigeon. Although the technology is tremendously advanced, the actual efficiency of the written word is no more powerful than it was two thousand years ago. Unless you are a careful, patient writer it is easy to write unclear and confusing emails. Moreover, it can be time-consuming: it can take half an hour to write an email that is the equivalent of a ten minute conversation on the telephone.

The difficulties are magnified when you are working with foreign providers. Their English is often very good, but they may use the language in a slightly different way from us, and have different cultural expectations. You can, of course, always pick up the telephone, but the quality of international lines, especially those in Asia, can still be surprisingly poor.

There are also questions of trust and loyalty. Working effectively with people demands strong relationships, which can be hard to form if your communication with your web developer or designer is based purely on email in his second language.

WI-FI AND ROAMING

If you do anything that is fundamentally based on communications, such as accounting, freelance writing and designing or consultancy work, it makes a lot of sense to be mobile and make the most of wireless internet (Wi-Fi) technology. Wireless-enabled laptop computers can be bought for not much more than £300, and can revolutionise the way you work.

A wireless network at home will allow you to work in the garden, in your bedroom or on the kitchen table. But the beauty of using Wi-Fi to run a roaming office is that you have a wider choice of where you are going to work. Armed with your laptop and a wireless connection you can work at home, in coffee shops, hotel foyers, a cottage in Devon, or by the pool in Spain.

At the moment, the only limitation on where you can work is that you need to have wireless coverage. At home, you simply need a broadband connection and a wireless router. Away from home, you have four basic options:

- The most popular and cheapest method is to sign up to a Wi-Fi provider that uses 'hotspots' (areas with wireless coverage) in public areas like pubs and coffee shops. The major UK providers are BT Openzone, T-Mobile and The Cloud.

19

- Many hotels and pubs have private Wi-Fi networks in public areas. A small number are free, but for most you will have to pay a fee on arrival. This is not necessarily the cheapest option, as it usually costs around £5 per session, but it is a good way to get connected if your regular Wi-Fi provider does not have a hotspot in the area.
- You can buy a special plugin modem for your computer and sign up to a 3G network, allowing you to use the internet wherever there is a phone signal. A number of UK telecoms providers are currently offering 3G modem packages, with varying features and limits on how much you can upload and download every month. 3G is not the cheapest way of connecting to the internet, but it can be convenient. Prices are likely to come down in the next few years as the competition becomes more intense.
- If you have a Bluetooth-enabled phone you can use it to connect your laptop to the internet. Most UK mobile providers offer this service, but as it tends to be very expensive, roaming workers usually use it only when there is no other option available.

When you are setting up a roaming office, you need to think about:

- **Security:** Identity theft has a high profile in the media. Most public Wi-Fi networks maintained by major suppliers are secure and password-protected; you need to make sure your home wireless connection is too. There are three different security standards.

The most common is WEP. Once it is set up, your own computers can automatically connect to your network, but anyone else would be prompted to enter your network password. Public connectivity is usually very secure, though if you have a Bluetooth connection you should adjust the security settings to reject connections from nearby computers unless they have your permission.

- **Speed:** The nearer you are to a wireless hub, the faster your connection. Walls and ceilings also have an impact.

Jargon Buster

Bluetooth A radio technology that allows mobile phones, computers and other electronic devices to exchange information.

3G The high-speed 'third generation' of mobile phone data networks.

Wireless hub A radio base station that allows nearby computers (usually within 100m) to access the internet wirelessly.

Bandwidth The amount of data you are allowed to download over your internet connection in a given time, usually a month.

WEP Short for Wired Equivalent Privacy, WEP is designed to provide the same level of security as that of a wired local area network. In practice it is not normally as secure as standard wired networks as these tend to also have physical security such as walls and ceilings.

Speed will be affected by the number of people sharing your connection. A secure network will prevent your neighbours from gaining free access to the net. When you are using Wi-Fi in public places, try to work out where the wireless hub is and sit close to it. Staff in wireless-enabled coffee bars, for example, will usually tell you where to sit to get the best reception.

- **Pricing and bandwidth:** If you are running a home wireless network, the most cost effective packages today are bundled offers from major broadband providers. If you are a high internet user and need to upload large files, you may be better off with a business package which has fewer users sharing the same connection and has high or unlimited bandwidth, allowing you to upload and download a very large amount of data. The other aspect to consider is the importance of your internet connection to your business and, therefore, how urgently you may need support. With a business package you have priority on customer service (within 24 hrs) compared to a consumer (3-5 days). Public Wi-Fi is rapidly getting cheaper, too, and a hotspot-based connection will generally offer unlimited bandwidth, providing you don't abuse it by downloading thousands of gigabytes of sound and video files. 3G networks are still the most expensive option for roamers, and tend to have tight restrictions on bandwidth. When you are buying an internet subscription of any sort, wired or wireless, always double-check the bandwidth allowance. Most providers market packages as having 'unlimited' bandwidth and then, in their fair usage policies, redefine the word 'unlimited' to include restrictions!

OFFICE EXPENSES AND TAX

Many of the costs associated with your office, whether it is based in your back bedroom, virtual or roaming, can be written off against tax. In fact, one of the many benefits of self-employment is that expenses you would have to pay for out of your pocket if you were employed, such as the cost of working at home in the evenings, are usually tax-deductible.

Currently you can offset a proportion of your home energy costs and local council tax against income tax. You can also include in your allowable expenses a proportion of the costs of converting your home for office use and any equipment required. The proportion will vary according to the type of expenditure, so it is worth talking to an accountant or tax adviser. In general, tax offsets against building work needs to phased over a ten year period while computer equipment would be phased over three years.

You will find HM Revenue and Customs very helpful when you start working for yourself and there is a wealth of useful information on their website, www.hmrc.gov.uk

Getting the right balance

One of the major challenges of the self-employed lifestyle is getting the balance between work and life right. This can be especially difficult if you are working from home.

Maintaining a good work-life balance is important. Even if you do not have a family, it is important to have a change of scene and a rest on a regular basis. When you first start out it can seem simple; the harder you work the more money you will make. Although true to an extent, you will soon find that working punishing hours has a diminishing returns effect. You become a less effective worker, more prone to mistakes. You can get to the point where you work so hard that your quality of work begins to suffer, perhaps leading to a damaged reputation and the loss of business.

Setting aside free time

Taking time out is so important that you should build it into your schedule. Although one of the pleasures of many types of self-employment is that you can work whenever you please, even at 2am if that is when you are sharp, you should try to have a particular routine for each working day, based on periods of work and rest.

Time management is also a crucial skill. If you work effectively and efficiently, you should not have to put in 20 hours a day. Here are some tips for managing your working time and ensuring that you own your business, rather than having it own you:

- **As far as possible, plan in advance.** We will look at medium to long-term planning in the next section, but day-to-day planning can be a huge timesaver. A good trick is to take five minutes at the end of every working day to plan the next, so when you hit the desk or get in your van the next morning you know exactly what you are doing.

- **Stay tidy.** There is nothing worse than losing an hour of your day looking for a particular tool or a cable for your laptop. Good organisation really pays off when it comes to filling in your yearly tax return. Many self-employed workers spend days fishing around in desk drawers, wallets and glove compartments for receipts and invoices. A little bit of advance planning and organisation can save a lot of time and heartache.

- **Farm out simple tasks to others.** Every small business has mundane jobs that need doing: envelopes need to be stuffed, websites updated, commercial vehicles cleaned. Tasks like these do

❝ Ring-fence time every day to spend with your family and loved ones. ❞

not need your skills, and it is probably more cost effective to pay someone else to do them. Many home workers swear by their domestic cleaners. Paying someone else to do the cleaning frees up your time and ensures you have a pleasant working environment, a double benefit for just a few pounds a week.

Family and social life

Self-employment can open up huge opportunities for your family, principally in the form of increased income and flexible working hours. But if you are not careful, it can do damage as well. The self-employed are notoriously prone to workaholism, and it is important not to let your work affect your relationships or the bringing up of your children.

It is crucial that you ring-fence time every day to spend with your family and loved ones. That doesn't mean just setting aside time to go to the supermarket or put up shelves, it means having quality free time.

When you are in full-time employment this is much easier, because there is a clear division between home and work. As a self-employed worker, you have to find time for your family.

Sometimes it is a question of not becoming over-focused on your business, and remembering the real reasons you work for yourself, which are probably tied up with increased freedom and income. It is not much use having lots of money and flexibility if you spend your life at your desk, or travelling from job to job.

Remember to relax

You need a social life, too. Another regular problem the self-employed come across is that they become so obsessed with their jobs they cannot forget about it, or talk about anything else. People tend to respect self-employed friends, and will often show interest in what you do, but remember not to take this as an invitation to bore them about your successes or burden them with your problems. When you are not working, try to forget about it altogether.

 Remember, hard work is not a virtue in itself. Although working for yourself is likely to be challenging and occasionally arduous, you should always impose a limit on the hours you work, if only because you need to rest and recuperate. If you work from home, it is also very easy to get 'cabin fever', the sudden and urgent desire to drop everything and escape from your desk.

Vision: you are what you plan

It is well worth taking some time to consider an aspect of running your own business that a surprising number of people forget: planning. Good planning will make the difference between success and struggle.

When you have your own business, more than ever before, your future is in your own hands. All of a sudden you can do whatever you want, for whoever you want, for a price that is decided by you. For some people this can be uncomfortable, there are no rules to hide behind. No-one is telling you what to do. Equally, your own productivity can be affected when nobody else is there managing your time. So it is absolutely critical that, when you work for yourself, you are disciplined about what you are doing.

You need to create your own goals, strategies, milestones and performance tests. Even if you do not construct a formal business plan, it is a good idea to decide upon these and write them down, that way you have got something concrete to aim at.

GOALS

These are the most important part of any plan, and you should have several of them: your daily goal might be simply to complete a list of tasks. In the medium term, you might focus on winning particular contracts and completing ones you have already taken on. Long term, you need to think about your financial and lifestyle goals.

All your planning should be built around the achievement of goals. A surprising number of self-employed individuals do not have any goals at all, but take everything on a day-to-day basis. This is living hand-to-mouth and, although it might seem easy, it doesn't offer the same rewards as working towards long-term goals and achieving them.

When you are setting your goals you need to strike a balance between being realistic and ambitious. It is unlikely that you are going to become a millionaire in your first year of work, but you can aim to earn a respectable income, perhaps in excess of what you received in your old job. You could also aim to build your business

&& You can do whatever you want, for whoever you want, for a price that is decided by you. &&

to a point where you are an established and respectable name in your field.

STRATEGIES

You need to decide upon the strategies you are going to follow in pursuit of your goals. Are you going to rely on referrals to win business, or launch an advertising campaign? Are you going to do all the work yourself, or farm it out to subcontractors, leaving you time to build your network and win new business?

The important thing about strategies is that they must be flexible. As you spend more time in self-employment you will accrue more experience and become better at finding out what works and what does not for your particular business. At first, you may have to learn by trial and error, which means adapting your strategies or changing them completely, as your business grows.

You should take strategy very seriously. Think very carefully about it, and try to be as concrete as possible. This, for example, is a weak strategy:

I'll attract business by building a website.

It is weak because it is vague. Try to be targeted. This would be much better:

I'll attract business by building a website that is designed to appeal to my core audience, young mothers. Just creating the site won't be enough. I'll drive traffic to it by being active in online forums, writing a blog, optimising the site for search engines and pursuing a campaign of print advertising in mother and baby magazines.

Planning point

Time-limited plans are better than open-ended ones, they demand focus and efficient work. If you do not incorporate milestones into your plan, you risk drifting. You may be working hard and thinking of good ideas, but not getting closer to your medium and long-term goals at a reasonable speed.

A strategy like that is precise and can act as the core of a plan. Importantly, it does not rely on a single technique for attracting customers and winning business. Instead, it incorporates a number of tactics. When the strategy is implemented you can build on the parts of it that move you effectively towards your goals and change or abandon those parts that are underperforming.

MILESTONES

It is important to include milestones in your planning. These are outlines of what you expect to have achieved, and by when. Clearly, when you are starting out in self-employment it can be difficult to assess timescales accurately, and milestones may have to be moved. However, as you become more experienced you will learn more about your capabilities and be able to time your projects accurately.

Milestones are useful for morale during long projects, when it can seem as if no end is in sight. If you are setting realistic deadlines that you miss regularly, you need to re-examine your strategies and working practices.

PERFORMANCE TESTING

Performance testing means looking at your business as you achieve particular goals and deciding how well you have performed in relation to what you set out to do. Some performance tests are easy: if one of your goals is to earn £30,000 in your first year, you only have to look at your accounts to see if you have passed or failed.

Like goals and strategies, performance tests need to be specific if they are to be useful. If you simply sit back and stare into space one afternoon and say to yourself, 'how am I getting on?' the answer you come up with is likely to be vague: 'OK, I suppose' or 'maybe I could do a bit better'.

Performance tests work best when they are demanding and are tied to particular goals:

- Have I earned my £15,000 target over the past six months?
- Have I added 8 medium-sized clients to my customer list?
- Have my profits increased by £8,000 since last year?
- Has my business grown by 20% over the past three years?
- Did I win at least one £20,000 contract?

If you pass your self-imposed performance tests, you owe yourself a pat on the back. If you fail any, you need to take a detailed look at why and amend your strategies accordingly.

Keeping track

You do not need to spend hours on your planning, but it should be something you think about regularly. Write down your plans and revisit them systematically. If you make plans and use them carefully, they can help your business enormously – allowing you to enjoy the benefits the self-employed lifestyle can offer.

What sort of business?

The type of self-employment you choose should be based on your skills and experience, the opportunities available and, most importantly, the presence of a relevant market. Before you start, define exactly what you are going to do and make sure that the business you choose is right for you.

Your business model

You may not be a multinational corporation but, just like one, you need a business model, a system for using your skills and products or services to make money.

Business models do not need to be complex, but it is important that you have a clear sense of yours before you launch your business. In this chapter we are going to look at three basic models:

- **Product sales** – selling products to customers for more than it costs you to create or acquire them.
- **Service** – using your skills and talents to do something for your customers that they either cannot do themselves or do not have time for.
- **Franchise** – buying a 'turnkey business' and running your own operation under its brand, using the parent company's marketing system and supply network.

Case Study Rick

Rick is a painter and decorator. He says: "There are lots of professional people in my area with young families. They don't have much spare time for decorating, so I do it for them. My customers buy the materials, and I do the work." Rick leaves his customers to choose and buy their own paint and wallpaper. He just provides brushes, cleaning materials and labour. His business model is based entirely on providing a service.

Case Study Rita

Rita is a self-employed florist, working from home. She says, "There's a shortage of florists in my area who specialise in arrangements, so I meet the market's demands by providing flowers for weddings, funerals and parties." It doesn't get much simpler than that. Rita is selling a product (the flowers), but she is also offering a service by using her knowledge and experience to provide arrangements and displays for different events.

It is also common for models to combine. For example, a self-employed plumber may sell showers and bathroom suites (product sales) as well as fitting them (service).

You will also find that as time goes on and you discover new opportunities, your model will change and grow. So we are also going to look at:

- **Creating your own model** – to fit the exact needs of your market.
- **Adding value** – basing your model on somebody else's product or service, and enhancing it.

Of course, any model must be based on a market for the product or service your business will provide. Ideally, you should identify a market and then decide how best to satisfy its needs. Some businesses flounder because they fail to identify a target market.

Case Study Andy

Andy works from home, building PCs. He explains: "I really enjoy gaming, and I know there's a demand for high-performance PCs that the major high street retailers and online suppliers aren't fulfilling. I buy components and build specialist gaming computers. I've built a very good reputation through word-of-mouth marketing. I also make money by helping gamers who are having technical problems with their PCs." Andy's basic business model is product sales. However, he's adding considerable value to the components he buys from manufacturers by turning them into high value computers. And because he is experiencing an increased demand for after-sales support and training, his model is evolving to include a service element.

Rick, Rita and Andy in our case studies all have a clear idea of how their businesses work and the markets they are aiming at. Before you become self-employed, so should you. It is not much use simply saying to yourself: "I'm going to be a web designer." That doesn't define your precise business or market. Are you going to design websites for start-ups or established businesses? Is your focus going to be on ecommerce? Is there a particular sector where you have specialist knowledge or skills?

Knowing your exact business model gives you a clear sense of where you are going. It is related to your goals and strategies, which we discussed in the last chapter, and is the basis of your marketing and expansion plans, which we will come on to later (see Chapter 7). Later in this chapter we are going to look at the opportunities and risks that different business models present.

Targeted thinking

- **When you are deciding on what form of self-employment to undertake, you should avoid thinking like this: "I like gardening; I'll become a landscaper."**
- **Rather, you should think something like this: "There are a lot of older houses in our town with large gardens. Most of these are owned by professional people who do not want to spend their weekends mowing the lawn. I can use my landscaping design skills to create easy-to-manage gardens. I can also provide an on-going maintenance service."**

The sort of business you start will be governed by your skills and experience. However, when you are creating your business model you should first consider the needs of your target market.

Selling products

Selling goods for a profit is probably the world's oldest way of doing business. To join this long-standing tradition, you will first need to work out where you are going to get your goods from and establish whether you will sell them through a shop or online.

Let us assume you have identified a market for a product. The first thing you have to deal with is sourcing; where is the stuff you sell going to come from?

The simplest method for sourcing products is to make them yourself. For example, if you are a self-employed artist, craftsman or cake maker, your business model is creating a product that you can sell. This type of business has three advantages:

- The transition from raw materials to a finished product sold direct to an end-user offers the best opportunity for profit.
- If you arrange trade terms with your suppliers and your customers pay you straight away, your exposure to cashflow problems is limited.
- You are the creator of the product, rather than a middleman. Increasingly manufacturers are using technology to sell direct to the end-user. If you are the manufacturer, you are not in that vulnerable position.

On the other hand, there are also some disadvantages:
- Making products takes time. If you spend most of your working hours baking cakes or painting pictures you are not leaving yourself much time for marketing and sales.
- The profit you make is limited by the amount of product you can manufacture. In this way, selling your own products is a bit like selling your skills as a service provider; your earnings are limited by the number of hours in a day.

Making and selling products is the basis of many 'hobby' businesses. If your priority is doing something you enjoy, rather than generating a significant income, a hobby business can be a very rewarding one.

However, unless you are going to operate on a large scale, or have a talent for turning water into wine, manufacturing your own products is never going to make you a fortune. A better alternative is to consider selling somebody else's products.

BUYING AND SELLING

Buying products from a manufacturer and selling them on is, if you like, a purer way of doing business than making your own products. It is also more efficient. You buy products at wholesale price from a specialist manufacturer and sell them

Case Study Charlie

Charlie has loved cycling since he was a child and, after leaving school, he learned how to make racing bikes. His business is based on making custom racers, measuring his customers like a tailor would measure them for a suit and creating frames that are exactly the right size. He has a UK-wide reputation and sells custom frames for well in excess of a thousand pounds. Unfortunately, it takes time to make a bike, and Charlie puts a lot of love and time into the creation of each frame. He is a happy guy and financially comfortable, but he is not rich. His ability to earn is limited by the amount of time it takes him to manufacture his products.

to the end-user for a profit. If you are dealing with a large manufacturer that can turn out products by the thousands, and you can find the customers, you can potentially make a lot of money.

Selling someone else's product also has risks:

- Depending on the lead time for orders, and how you sell your products (can you sell from a brochure or via a website?), you may need to carry stock. This generally means paying suppliers for products before your customers have paid you. This can lead to cashflow problems.
- With the development of the internet, many manufacturers are now selling direct

to end-users. Unless you 'add value' to the products you resell, there is a risk of being cut out of the supply chain.

❝ A hobby business can be a very rewarding one. ❞

Case Study Tony

Tony is a great cyclist, but not much good with his hands. So when he started his business he decided to buy in bikes from well-known suppliers and sell them on. Because he is buying stock he has to manage his cashflow carefully, but he does not spend ages making products. The result is that Tony sells ten or fifteen bikes a week. Although Tony is only making a margin on the bikes he sells, after all he has to buy them to start with, he earns nearly twice as much as Charlie (in the above case study) because of the sheer volume of products he is managing to shift. Because someone else is making the bikes for him, he can focus all his energy on sales and marketing, leading to greater profits.

Cashflow is a major concern for any business and a whole subject to itself. We are going to take a detailed look at cashflow management strategies in Chapter 10. But before we go any further, it is worth taking a detailed look at how to deal with the pitfalls of being a middleman.

Piggy in the middle

Twenty years ago, if you were the sole importer of a product manufactured on the other side of the world, you pretty much had a captive market. With the advent of the internet, it is much easier for consumers to buy directly from manufacturers direct, rather than dealing with intermediate sellers. Many manufacturers are changing the way they do business to fit this trend, with major players like Dell computers exploiting the power of the internet to sell the products they manufacture direct to consumers.

However, if you choose the right products to sell and develop a positive attitude to customer relationships and marketing, you can reduce or eliminate these risks. Here are some basic strategies that should get you off to a good start:

- Build strong relationships with suppliers that can offer the right product at the right price, but who do not want to get involved in the hassle and expense of dealing with customers direct.
- Add value to a product that its producer is not in a position to add. The classic way is to offer a high level of after-sales support. A manufacturer in Shanghai might be able to sell products direct to consumers in the UK, but it is not in a position to support them after the sale.
- Develop a reputation. If customers know you as a dealer they can trust for good advice and customer care, they will be willing to pay a bit extra than they would have to if dealing with the manufacturer direct.

SELLING ON THE INTERNET

Before we move on from product sales, it is worth considering a couple of the new opportunities the internet has brought to the marketplace: affiliate marketing and eBay trading.

The concept of earning commissions for sales has been around for years, but the internet has made it much easier. You can generate an income promoting Amazon's books and DVDs or sell online music through Apple's iTunes store. Affiliate programmes allow you to generate commissions selling a whole range of products from bathrooms, fridges, computers and mobile phones through to mortgages. Although commissions are lower than if you were handling the

Jargon Buster

Affiliate marketing Using the internet to promote someone else's products without having to buy or hold any stock yourself. Everything remains with the manufacturer or main dealer, who handles the payment process and shipping and pays you a commission for every sale you make.

Jargon Buster

eBay The website www.ebay.com, which allows people all over the world to buy and sell new and used items to one another.

Building an online business takes time and effort. Internet selling can make good returns, as long as you take time to study the markets and accept that you are not going to succeed overnight. Take time out to research, but be wary that while there are scores of ebooks about how to make easy money on the internet, many are sold by people who generate an income selling books and do not necessarily have the 'been there and done it' knowledge.

items direct, there is no risk and no physical limit to your earning potential. The main secret of affiliate success is to develop an understanding of the products you are promoting; that's the only way you're going to build a quality website that attracts visitors. A classic example of a successful affiliate site would be www.uswitch.com. Free information attracts visitors who, on making a decision, click on an affiliate link generating a commission payment to the site.

Trading on eBay is somewhat similar, except it usually involves the physical handling of goods. You can use eBay.com to sell your own products, of course, but most eBay traders source products cheaply, sometimes from the eBay marketplace itself, and sell them on at a profit.

As with affiliate marketing, product knowledge and an eBay reputation will increase your ability to generate business. By concentrating on a particular sector, you will develop the ability to spot good prices and pitch your products to eBay's (usually rather savvy) buyers.

For more detailed information about doing business online, see Chapter 8.

Selling services

Selling a service is very different from selling a product, both in terms of the way you market your offer to clients, and the way you manage your own time.

If you are a self-employed specialist, your time and skills are valuable commodities that clients are willing to pay for. Although there are plenty of people with saleable skills, many of them are tied up in full-time employment, and buyers can struggle to find skilled, reliable individuals who have the flexibility to work on short or medium term contracts.

Providing there is a need for the service you offer and you market yourself effectively, you have every chance of establishing yourself in business. There are very few parts of the service sector that have enough specialists to meet the demands of the markets. This is particularly obvious in what used to be called the 'trades'; electrics, plumbing, joinery, plastering and related skills.

However, it is also true that there is a lack of good quality service providers in the so-called knowledge economy. If you are a genuinely good web designer, for example, you should have no problem finding work.

THE ADVANTAGES

If you are genuinely good at what you do, you are willing to work hard and you are offering a service to meet an identified demand, you should find starting a business reasonably straightforward. However, any business takes time to establish a reputation, so you should plan your finances to cope with slow but gradual growth.

Keeping down costs

As a service provider, unless you need specialist equipment, your start-up costs and overheads are generally lower than if you are selling products.

It is worth remembering that expenses, such as those illustrated in our case studies, are tax-deductible, although not completely so in the case of household bills and car costs. If your turnover is in excess of £65,000 per year, you also need to be VAT registered. If the majority of your clients are registered, it may well be in your interest to register too, even if your turnover is below the threshold, (see Chapter 3).

Flexibility

The other major benefit of being a self-employed service provider is that your business is very flexible. It is much easier to change a service-based enterprise than a product-based one, as you don't need to liquidate your stocks or risk additional investment.

Most freelance service providers find that their businesses change and grow over time. After a few years working in a specialist field you will find that your experience and contacts become as valuable, if not more so, than the actual work you do. For example, if you are a project manager who specialises in new energy projects, you will find that you develop close relationships with key people across the sector. You can exploit this network to develop your business.

In fact, if you are going into the service sector, you should work hard to expand your network. You should also, as your experience grows, consider contracting work out or recruiting staff. This helps

Case Study   June

June runs a small domestic cleaning business. She has a number of regular customers in the small market town where she lives, and walks between jobs. There are a couple of customers in villages outside of town, and she travels to them in her car. June usually turns over £210 every week. She uses her customers' own cleaning equipment but brings along products like polish, bleach and cleaning cloths, which she can buy cheaply from a supplier. Her weekly expenses are quite low: £10 per week on fuel for work journeys in her car and £25 per week on cleaning products. She also has miscellaneous expenses but her total costs rarely exceed £40 a week, leaving her with a net profit of £170.

Case Study   Tariq

Tariq's work involves different projects, from raising capital for technology companies to running small ecommerce businesses. He has a home office, but spends a lot of time visiting clients. From his fees and sales he generally earns around £1,400 per week. However, he also has many expenses. He spends around £80 per week on petrol. His car is mostly used for business purposes, so costs like the purchase finance, maintenance and road tax are partial business expenses. Over a year, he spends £8,000 on car costs, averaging out at £160 per week. His home office costs around £35 per week to run, including broadband, heating, lighting and stationery, plus £25 per week for his mobile phone. And because he is often away from home, accommodation and dining expenses average around £100 per week. That is £320 of weekly expenses, making Tariq's net profit somewhere in the region of £1,025 per week.

to address one of the problems of the service model, the difficulty of expansion.

THE DISADVANTAGES

Being a self-employed service provider is not all fun and games. There are certain problems common to the sector, and, whether you are a childminder, tutor, builder or graphic designer, you will probably run into all of them to a greater or lesser extent.

Time is money

If you are selling a product, the profit you make is only limited by the number you can sell. If you have a million mousetraps to sell, and a million people are each willing to pay £5 for one, you can turn over five million pounds.

If, on the other hand, you are a service provider charging £25 an hour, you are going to have to fit 40,000 hours into your day to make the same amount, and that is not going to happen. As a service provider the amount you earn is limited by the number of hours you can work. As your business develops you can get around this problem by working through others and subcontracting. However, for your first few years at least, there will be a definite cap on your earnings. It might be quite a high cap, but it is a cap all the same.

Getting the run around

The other disadvantage of being a service provider is that you are more likely to be messed about by clients. This can take the form of changed specifications on work that has already been completed, or failure to settle invoices.

Difficulties like this can be common if you are working on short-term contracts in the information economy, such as writing, design or administrative services. Such work is often carried out remotely, so briefs are not always as clear as they should be, and it is common for client businesses in this sector to have cashflow problems of their own. If you are going to survive as an information service provider, it is important to define the exact nature of the work, terms and conditions before you begin a contract. This is best achieved through a simple service agreement.

This is not a complex contract but a simple document that outlines the work you agree to do and the timescale. You also need to write down exactly what is included in the price you are charging (for example, the number of revisions to a web design) and what is extra, as well as your terms for payment and any penalties for late settlement of invoices.

When you present the service agreement to your client, make a point of highlighting the benefits: it does, after all, clarify the situation for both parties. You can also use a working version of the document as a basis for agreeing a definite brief for the work you are going to deliver.

You will have less difficulty if you are doing a more practical job, such as servicing cars. Payment generally appears pretty quickly if your client realises he is not going to be getting the keys to his Jaguar back until he hands over the cash!

 For a more detailed look at the tax and VAT implications of the self-employed lifestyle see Chapter 3.

Franchising and combined models

Finally in this chapter, we are going to look at franchising and some of the ways you can combine classic business models to create an operation that is uniquely yours.

Many people want their own business but do not want to be on their own. For those that have the capital, buying a franchise is an option worth considering. In 2007 in the UK, there are 781 franchise opportunities, employing more than 370,000 people. The more established the core business, the higher the price of the franchise. At their peak, franchises of the fast food restaurant chain, McDonald's, could cost several hundred thousand pounds. At the other end of the scale, a relatively unproven children's party franchise could be yours for under £10,000.

THE ADVANTAGES

A franchise is a turnkey business. This means it is a proven business that is ready to run, with systems, business support, marketing methods and stock availability all wrapped in a business model that meets the needs of an identified niche market. In most cases good franchise businesses allow you to focus on the operations of the business. You do not need to get involved in strategy or creating the day-to-day processes. They are decided for you, all you have to do is follow the rules.

Participating in an established business model can make it easier to raise finance, recruit staff and find premises. It is also more likely to attract customers and secure higher prices.

THE DISADVANTAGES

Buying a franchise will require an up-front fee plus an annual royalty fee that is usually linked to a percentage of sales.

As a franchisee you have less freedom than someone running a business that is wholly their own. If you are creative you may find this frustrating. Because the

 For further information on franchises and for help in making an informed decision about franchising, see the British Franchise Association website, www.thebfa.org

success of a franchise is based on duplication, most are very restrictive in terms of what they allow you to do. This can prevent you from introducing a new marketing initiative, developing a new product or service, or trading in a different area. If business takes a dive, there is little you can do to take radical action without the approval of the franchise company.

You can often get caught in the middle. You know you have a problem, and you may even have the solution, but you cannot take action without specific authorisation to do so.

OTHER OPTIONS

One of the great things about starting-up is that you can choose any business model you like, as long as it fits the needs of an available market.

In Chapter 1 we talked about the possibilities of running a portfolio career. This type of approach is ideal if you

Case Study   Mike

Mike is an ex-public health official with specialist knowledge in smoking. Having spent twenty years working for a local authority, he has taken voluntary redundancy and has started a business advising large organisations on formulating and enforcing smoking policies and how best to support members of staff who wish to quit. In addition to finding his own clients, Mike has joined an established health and safety consultancy firm as an associate, and is helping them to exploit the growing cultural and legislative agenda surrounding smoking. The company finds the work and pays Mike a daily rate for contracts.

wish to mix and match work across a variety of models and sectors, allowing you to be both a seller of products and a service provider. The downside to a portfolio approach is that it is easy to spread yourself too thinly. Trying to be a Jack of all trades can result in you losing focus on long-term goals. It is hard to achieve a single, major goal without giving it the majority of your effort and attention.

Another common half-way point between models is an associate relationship. This allows self-employed workers to trade as if they were employed by a company without restricting their ability to trade as themselves. It also allows the company to increase its capacity as and when required, without the need for long term commitment.

Case Study   Jane

Jane has just left her role as a Senior Staff Trainer in a multinational company. She would like to establish a business running corporate team building programmes, but lacks the materials and the track record to appeal to her target customers.

She decides to purchase a regional licence from an international training franchise that works in the UK corporate market. The franchise company has everything in place for her, including the materials for the training programmes she will deliver, a full marketing system and established service partners to meet needs such as insurance and printing. With all this in place, Jane is confident her contacts and experience will enable her to secure the contracts she needs.

Getting the basics right

Before you launch your business you need to make some decisions about structure and get your tax situation organised. None of it is complicated – but it has to be done!

Dealing with tax

You can save yourself a lot of time and money by understanding the way the tax system works and your place within it. In this section we are going to look at how to get off to a good start with Her Majesty's Revenue and Customs.

INFORMING THE TAX OFFICE

You need to inform your local tax office within three months of starting a business. This can be done by completing a CWF1 form available from HM Revenue & Customs (HMRC), by visiting www.hmrc.gov.uk and registering online, or by calling the Helpline for the Newly Self-Employed 08459 15 45 15. This establishes the correct relationship with 'the Revenue' from the start and also means you will avoid having to pay a £100 penalty for late registering. Once you are registered you will be able to begin the management of your taxes and National Insurance.

If you have recently left an employed position, sending your P45 to your tax inspector will help ensure you get your correct allowance. Also if you start self-employment in, say, September after being in full-time employment since April (the start of the tax year), it is likely that you have overpaid some tax and are due

a refund. HMRC will usually give you the option of leaving the refund on account to offset against your next tax bill, though if you could use the cashflow they will pay it to you direct.

Jargon Buster

P45 The document you receive from your former employer to confirm you have ceased to work for that company.

PAYING TAX AND NATIONAL INSURANCE

It is important to consider the taxman as soon as you become self-employed. In contrast to being an employee, where income tax and National Insurance (NI) are automatically deducted through the PAYE system, when you become self-employed you need to organise paying your tax by yourself. So when the

To find your local tax office look in the phone book under HM Revenue & Customs, or the department's former name 'Inland Revenue'. Alternatively use the 'contact us' button on the www.hmrc.gov.uk website, choose the Enquiry Centres option and enter your location for a list of your nearest offices.

taxman does ask for his money it is important to be prepared. Ideally, you should build in a method of saving for your tax bill when it falls due. However, when you become self-employed, you will get a period of grace before your first payment is due. And while this initial period of self-employment allows you to use your gross income, the tax still needs to be paid, so get saving!

The bad news is that although you have got up to 23 months before you actually pay your first tax bill, when it lands it will be a demand for the equivalent of 18 months' tax. This is the tax due for your first year's business, for example 2008/2009 plus an additional payment of 50 per cent of that figure on account for the year 2009/2010. You then pay a balancing payment at the end of July, and according to your tax return, continue make payments every six months thereafter.

Your tax return

Your tax return will need to include the supplementary pages for self-employment. If you have already advised your local tax office of your status and have registered for Class 2 National Insurance Contributions (see overleaf) this will happen automatically.

If your annual turnover is less than £15,000 you only need to complete a short tax return. This four-page document is less complex than the standard one and only requires you to enter turnover, total expenses and profit.

Although technology has made completing your tax return much easier, it is worthwhile using an accountancy service to provide you with advice and guidance. Their experience can help you reduce your tax bill, ensure that you allocate your costs correctly and reclaim any tax previously overpaid.

When your tax should be paid during your first two years of operation

Operation	When	
Self-employment	begins April 2008	* HMRC will calculate your tax liability if your completed return is received by 30 Sept.
Tax return	issued April 2009	
Tax return – first deadline	return by 30 Sept 2009*	
Tax return – final deadline	return by 31 Jan 2010	** After the payment on 31 July, payments are then made every six months.
Payment due – Yr 1 plus 50% of Yr 2	31 Jan 2010	
Payment due – 50% of Yr 2	31 July 2010**	

Fred has been made redundant by his engineering company. He has been there for 13 years and is entitled to one week's payment for each year he has been employed. This comes to £2,990. He is also contractually obliged to receive 13 weeks' notice but, as the factory is closing, his company is paying him in lieu. Because he is being made redundant he can receive both these payments free of tax and NI. As it is October, he is also half-way through a tax year, so he is likely to receive a partial tax refund for the period April-October.

If your business is complex, or growing rapidly, an on-going relationship with an accountant could pay dividends. Although it is not really necessary to pay professional fees for basic administration work, financial advice at the right level can make significant difference to any business.

National Insurance

There are two main types of National Insurance Contributions (NICs), collected by the National Insurance Contributions Office (NICO). If you are earning in excess of £5,225 you will need to pay Class 2 National Insurance (NI) a flat weekly contribution of £2.20 per week (from

April 07). This is generally paid by direct debit or can be paid in cash at the Post Office. You are also liable for a Class 4 payment in proportion to your profits above a minimum threshold of £5,225 and an upper level of £34,840. The current rate is 8%. Class 4 NICs are assessed in your tax return and the payment due included in your final bill.

VAT

VAT registered businesses charge the tax on their products and services and then forward it to HMRC on a quarterly or annual basis. In other words, if you are registered for VAT, you are essentially acting as a tax collector for the government. The upside is that you can offset the VAT you pay on supplies against the VAT you collect on sales.

You must register for VAT if your turnover is more than £65,000 (from April 07). Alternatively, you can voluntarily register for VAT when your turnover is below that threshold if you believe it is in your business interests. You might choose to do this if:

NICO National Insurance Contributions Office, the part of HM Revenue & Customs that deals with the collection and recording of National Insurance contributions.

VAT Invented by the French in 1954, Value-Added Tax is a tax charged at the point of sale on all sales made on eligible items within the UK.

❝If you inform HMRC at the start, you will avoid having to pay a £100 penalty for late registering.❞

- Your business needs a lot of VAT-registered supplies.
- You want to allow your customers to reclaim the VAT element of your invoice.
- You want to give your operation the reputation for permanence that VAT rating gives in the eyes of other businesses.

It is easy to make the mistake of thinking that registering for VAT means your prices automatically increase by 17.5%. That element certainly relates to work where you are just charging for your time, but if you buy and sell VAT-registered products you will already be paying VAT on all purchases which you are having to pass onto your customers. VAT registration allows you, effectively, to take VAT out of the equation.

To assist small businesses in reducing the administration and the burden of quarterly returns, there are different schemes available, including the Flat Rate Scheme, the Annual Accounting Scheme and the Cash Accounting Scheme.

Flat-rate VAT

The Flat Rate Scheme allows you to calculate your VAT due as a percentage of your sales. This varies according to your business type, for example, for secretarial services it is 11%, for hairdressing 12%. To qualify for the flat rate scheme your turnover must be less than £150,000.

Case Study   John

John runs a commercial portable heating business from his home. Most of his customers are businesses. Although his turnover of £42,000 is below the £65,000 threshold, he is considering registering for VAT.

John's costs are about £21,000, which includes approximately £3,000 in VAT. If VAT-registered he would need to charge an additional 17.5% on his sales, but as his customers are mostly VAT-rated businesses they can reclaim this on their own VAT returns.

John would need to charge VAT of approximately £7,350 on his £42,000 sales. Although this means more paper work, it also means that he would be better off because he could reclaim the £3,000 he has paid in VAT. John has not only improved his net profit by £3,000, by having a company which is VAT-registered he has also raised his credibility with business customers.

❝If you are registered for VAT, you are essentially acting as a tax collector for the government.❞

To contact NICO by post you should write to: National Insurance Contributions Office, CAAT, Longbenton, Newcastle upon Tyne NE98 1ZZ. You may also call the helpline on 0845 302 1479.

Annual Accounting Scheme

The Annual Accounting Scheme allows you to make a set VAT payment each month or every quarter. You also only complete one VAT return at the end of the year. Whilst this can reduce your paperwork, there is the danger that by removing the discipline of regular accounting you may fall behind with your books, which can lead to all sorts of problems.

Cash Accounting Scheme

If you invoice clients and are likely to face delays in payments, you can opt for the Cash Accounting Scheme whereby you account for VAT on the basis of payments you receive and make, rather than on invoices you issue and receive. The main benefit of this scheme is that it helps your cashflow, particularly if your customers pay you late, although it also means you cannot reclaim VAT on purchases until you pay your suppliers.

 For further information on VAT, including the Flat Rate Scheme, see http://customs.hmrc.gov.uk or call the National Advice Service on 08450 10 90 00.

Business structure

When setting up your business, in addition to dealing with tax, you need to think about the legal structure your business will take: sole trader, limited company or partnership.

Each of the main structures have their advantages and disadvantages. Most self-employed individuals who do not employ staff or run complex businesses are sole traders. However, there may be advantages to forming a company or a partnership. In this section we will take a look at each structure in turn and think about what it could offer your business.

Sole trader

Setting up as a sole trader is very easy. It is the structure most commonly used by self-employed workers who deliver services to the public or other small businesses. The administration is very simple and there are few onerous accounting rules.

On the downside you are personally responsible for any debts your company has. If the worst happens you could be made bankrupt and your personal assets (your house, for example) sold to pay your creditors.

Limited company

A limited company is responsible for its own debts. If, for example, your business involves wholesale buying and selling, it could only take one major customer failing to pay a large invoice to land you in trouble. In that kind of situation, becoming a limited company would be a better option than

Case Study **Jane**

Jane runs a project management events business. She negotiates best prices with hotels, events and travel companies, but her clients settle the accounts direct. She charges a daily rate for managing the actual event and earns an agency commission paid from any organisations she places bookings with. Her customers are all large, blue chip companies, so although payments for her services occasionally slip, they are always paid.

Jane has one member of staff, works from her home office and has little exposure to risk. She operates as a sole trader, judging that in her case the minor benefits of forming a limited company aren't worth the extra administrative hassle.

remaining a sole trader. If things go wrong, the company goes bust: you don't, as long as you can establish that you have run the operation legally and in good faith.

Limited companies, like VAT registration, can also add to your credibility if you are dealing with other businesses. On the downside, you are required to submit annual accounts to Companies House and there is an increased level of administration and government regulation to deal with.

However, starting a limited company does not let you have your cake and eat it; you cannot freely borrow money without taking responsibility for the debt. Particularly in the early years, lenders may still seek personal security from you, the director. Depending on the value of your company and the length of time you've been trading, a personal guarantee, usually in the form of your house, will be required for any loans.

Case Study   Terry & Harry

Terry and Harry's kitchen design and installation business is a shining example of a successful partnership. Terry's skills are in fitting and managing the installations, while Harry is the designer and partner responsible for winning new business.

Starting as a two-man band working out of Terry's garage, they kept costs low, and after a year had the funds to open a high street studio to promote their premium kitchen range. Harry worked with a local graphic designer to brand the business and create superb designs. Terry focused on developing a team of high-quality fitters (themselves self-employed) who shared the partnership's passion for exacting standards.

By working together, they established a business that they would have struggled to grow on their own. And now that their business has grown again, they have formed a Limited Liability Partnership (LLP).

Case Study   Bill

Bill is a trader. His core business is a range of branded sportswear, which he sources direct from manufacturers and other dealers. He buys large parcels of products and breaks them up before selling them direct to retailers and smaller dealers. His business is high volume and as a middleman he makes a relatively small margin on each transaction. He is consistently exposed to the risk of bad debt. Bill opts to form a limited company. While there is still the risk that one of his customers will not pay him, he is not personally liable in the way that he would be as a sole trader.

Partnerships

It is common for start-ups to consider a partnership arrangement. From a standing start, the idea of sharing the risk or the responsibility of making things work can be attractive, but it is an approach that should be taken with care.

Partnerships will only work if all partners share the same goals and actively work together to achieve them. You do not have to agree about everything, in fact, constructive discussion and analysis of each others' views is likely to result in a more focused strategy.

A partnership does not have to be for life. Some businesses start out as a simple partnership, but then choose to become incorporated or to change status to a limited liability partnership at a later stage when cashflow allows for the cost of registration and legal support.

As a partnership, the approach and attitude you take to work is much more important than if you are a sole trader. You, as an individual, will lose a certain amount of control over your business, everything has to be done as an equal team. There is nothing more galling than one partner doing all the work, while the other sits back and does next to nothing.

Jargon Buster

Limited Liability Partnership (LLP)
A business structure that operates under the limited liability of an ordinary limited company while retaining the structure of a partnership.

❝ Having a life partner who is also a business partner can work outstandingly well. ❞

FAMILY BUSINESSES

Share your life, share your business. Having a life partner who is also a business partner can work outstandingly well. It can also go very wrong.

Perhaps some of the most important qualities to look for in any relationship are trust, understanding and common goals. If you already have those attributes in a marriage or life partnership, you already have a clear advantage over the majority. The question is, can you transfer those special qualities into a business arrangement?

The upsides

During start-up, in particular, having an understanding and supportive partner can make a massive difference to getting through tough times.

Life and business partnerships can also work well if one of the partners takes care

of the finance. Too often businesses fail because finance is not managed properly. Entrepreneurs have absolute belief in themselves and often chase dreams without thinking them through, failing to tell their partners about the financial risks in the process. This puts even greater pressure on the partner to deliver, which if it all works out is fine, but when things start to go wrong can lead to business and relationship problems. Having two of you in the business keeps everything on track and everyone aware of exactly what the financial situation is at any one time. There is perhaps a little less pressure to 'bring home the bacon' for your spouse, as he or she is directly

Planning point

In England, Wales and Northern Ireland, each partner is equally responsible for any debt owed by the partnership. In Scotland, partners are both jointly and severally liable for their partnership's debt. This means that they are responsible for both their own share of the debt and also for the partnership's entire debt. In each jurisdiction, your personal assets may be used to settle the debts of your business.

involved in the business with you.

One of the other major benefits of a family business is the level of organisation that partners with different skills can bring. Organised businesses are more in control and better prepared to succeed. If your life partner keeps you on track, increasing your effectiveness, then your business will ultimately do better than if you were running it by yourself, or in partnership with someone who doesn't know you so well.

You will also be well aware of one another's strengths and weaknesses. Confidence is one of the most important aspects of business. If your life partner is supportive and encourages you to succeed, then that is a major advantage. If you are both involved in the business and can constructively criticise and respond to each other, that is another bonus.

The disadvantages

Launching a business takes time and it means taking risks. If one of you sticks with a regular job and a guaranteed salary covering the basic household costs, it will provide time for a new business to establish itself. Having no guaranteed income between you increases the drive to succeed, but it also it also cranks up the stress and the likelihood that you'll fall out.

❝ A guaranteed salary, covering the basic household costs, provides time for a new business to establish itself. ❞

> **!** You cannot operate 24 hours a day. When your life partner is also involved in the business, it is not so easy to escape. Your business and your home life become completely tangled up. You need to have a very high tolerance for each other if you're going to make it work.

Sometimes you need support from people who are not directly involved. If your life partner is your business partner, you automatically lose a trusted person who stands outside the business who you can go to when times are tough.

BUSINESSES WITH FRIENDS

Similar to setting up in business with a life partner, going into business with a friend has its attractions. You enjoy each others' company, so why not make money together?

The big difference between friends and life partners is how you split the benefits. If you share your life with someone, there is a reasonable chance you share the bank account, so you can be flexible about how things are going work out in the long term. With friends things are different, and much more thought needs to be given to how you allocate responsibilities and rewards.

You also need to accept the possibility that your business may be the ruination of your friendship, and not only if things go wrong. People you think you know well can become very different when you are dealing with money. If you are thinking about starting this sort of partnership, you need to agree, in detail, in advance, exactly who is going to do what and who is going to be paid what.

Case Study | Linda and John

Linda and John formed a web design company when their employer went into liquidation. Retaining some of the previous business's clients gave them a platform to build on. Linda, the designer, maintained relationships and delivered award-winning designs. John's role was to generate new business.

Six months into the partnership they started to struggle. John's new clients didn't match the agreed profile, margins were tighter than expected and Linda had to work around the clock to maintain standards. It soon became apparent that John did not share Linda's views on account management. To make things worse, he was a strictly nine-to-five worker. Things came to a head one weekend when John wasn't prepared to work late to put an important tender together. Linda's designs were ready, but John failed to complete the written presentation by the deadline.

They agreed to part company. John found work in a new company and Linda continued to work as a freelance designer. The partnership was fairly simple to dissolve due to the fact that they weren't making any money. Linda took on responsibility for their overdraft in exchange for John relinquishing any future claims on the trading name and the few profitable customers he had introduced. It took three months of hard work to re-establish her credibility but with lower overheads she managed to make enough to survive and now has a thriving business serving clients that match her original profile.

Your home office

Even if you spend most of your time out and about, you are still going to need a base for doing paperwork, checking email and storing documents. If you do not have business premises, some sort of home office is essential, but it does not need to be expensive or difficult to set up.

In this section we are going to focus on the best way to set up and manage an office in the comfort of your own home. In some ways, this can be more difficult than working from business premises, and not only because it can blur the boundaries between your work and your home life.

LOCATION

The first thing you need to decide is exactly where in your home you are going to put your office. It is a very good idea to have a set space for this: although wireless connectivity and mobile telephones make it easy to set up shop on the kitchen table, you will quickly find that creating a separation between your business and home life can help to avoid unnecessary stress. In any case, it will not be long before you accumulate paperwork that needs to be organised and stored. If you are working for yourself full-time, the sort of commitment you are making really demands a space of its own.

Even if you live in a fairly small home, you can be imaginative about finding space for your office. You do not necessarily need

a whole room; some home offices are squeezed into spaces beneath staircases or on landings. This is not perfect if you are going to be spending a lot of time at your desk, but if you are only using office space for administration and spending the rest of your time away from home, it should be perfectly adequate.

Ideally, you should seek to use a room that gets a good amount of natural light during the day. It is also important to consider the temperature. It is not much fun typing in gloves during the winter.

❝ Even if you live in a fairly small home, you can be imaginative about finding space for your office. ❞

Conversions

If you are taking on a self-employed role requiring a great deal of desk time, you will find a dedicated office a considerable benefit to your business. A spare bedroom can be ideal for this. Alternatively, you could do what many other home workers have done and convert a garage, a summerhouse, a loft or a cellar for use as your office. If you take this route, make sure you get the job done properly: it is all very well using your cellar as an office, but if it is damp and dark you are unlikely to want to spend time there, which defeats the whole purpose of having a home office. Equally, do not neglect health and safety. If you choose to work in a shed at the bottom of the garden, remember to get the electricity supply and wiring checked out by a certified electrician.

If you really want to splash out, and your garden is big enough, you can have an office built. Several firms specialise in creating 'garden offices' with prices usually starting at around £4,000. Clearly, this is a major investment you may not want to make at the start of a self-employed career, though if you do have a large garden it can be worth considering later on, especially as it allows a degree of separation between your home and your office.

FURNITURE

If you are going to be spending a lot of time in your home office, it is worth investing in furniture designed for the purpose. Using any old desk and chair might seem the obvious, cheap option, but you can run into problems if you do not make these choices carefully.

Out-of-town retailers can offer fantastic value. If you are prepared to fetch, carry and use a screwdriver, it is possible to furnish your office for just a few hundred pounds. Alternatively, if you are after a more traditional look and feel, it is well worth considering specialist second-hand office furniture dealers that often offer high quality used furniture for a similar budget.

❝ In your working environment, comfort is not a luxury but a necessity. ❞

In your working environment, comfort is not a luxury but a necessity. Ending up with back problems or neck strain as a result of poor seating, or a desk that is the wrong height, can cause difficulty further down the line. If you are seated for more than an hour or two a day, you are at increased risk of encountering this sort of poor health. You do not want to be lying on the floor of your office trying to straighten out your back out when you should be talking to clients on the telephone.

Planning point

Lumbar support is particularly important. A chair than conforms to standard BS/EN/ISO 9241-5 is ideal, as it will help you keep your spine in the optimal position as you sit. Bear in mind that just because a chair is described as 'ergonomic' in its marketing materials, does not necessarily mean it conforms to this standard. A truly ergonomic chair will not be cheap and it may not be something you can afford in the early days of your business, but if you are going to be spending a lot of time sitting down, or you suffer from a back problem, it is one of the most important investments you can make.

If you are going to spend a long time sitting, the most important investment you can make is a well designed office chair. If your budget is tight it is worth considering an ex-corporate chair from an office dealer rather than a cheap new one. While a new, low-cost chair may look attractive, it is very likely that you will be more comfortable in a chair that is designed with ergonomics in mind.

Desks are much more a matter of personal choice, though it is a good idea to have one that offers you the maximum space possible for spreading out documents. Make sure it is the right height, too. When you sit with your office chair raised to a level where both feet are still flat on the ground, the edge of your desk should be approximately level with your elbows.

We will consider your physical wellbeing again shortly in the section on Repetitive Strain Injury (RSI). However, a point that we will make with relation to RSI is also worth making here: remember to take regular breaks from sitting. That does not have to be a break from work, if you have a cordless telephone you can take calls while you are walking around, and you can read paperwork while lying on the sofa. Try not to keep your backside on your seat for more than an hour at a time without taking a few minutes' break. Getting a stiff neck or sore back can severely affect your ability to concentrate.

STORAGE

Now that many documents are sent back and forth by email and, in many cases, never exist in a printed copy, there is a greatly reduced need for office storage.

However, you are always going to have some paperwork.

Paperwork to be managed

- **Your accounts and tax records.**
- **Your expense receipts.**
- **Invoices you have received from suppliers.**
- **Copies of invoices you have sent out to customers.**
- **Insurance certificates.**
- **Spare marketing material.**
- **Printed correspondence.**
- **Stationery.**

It is worth taking time to set up a filing system, even if it is a fairly general one. The best time to do this is before you start trading, it will save time and trouble later on, when you need to be focusing on making money.

If your business generates relatively little paperwork, a good quality, expanding file will probably do the job. If you are sending and receiving paper invoices, or you have to store printed materials, a good, old-fashioned filing cabinet are ideal and are far superior to their flat pack equivalent. These are either best purchased new from a specialist stationery supplier ('own brand' models offer better value) or from second hand dealers.

As well as traditional filing cabinets, there are all kinds of other storage solutions on the market. If you are working from home, the balance between functionality and aesthetics can be very important, so remember to involve partners and families when you are choosing equipment and setting up your office. This can also be a way of involving them in your business at an early stage.

COMPUTER EQUIPMENT

Technology is cheaper and more functional than it has ever been, so it makes absolute sense to take full advantage of it. If you are already working in a field that makes extensive use of information technology

(IT), the chances are that you have a good idea of your computer requirements. However, if your computer is a useful tool for your business rather than something that is absolutely central, it is worth thinking about how to get the best setup for your needs and the best possible value. For most people, the choices are relatively simple: desktop or notebook (laptop); Macintosh or Windows.

Desktops vs. Notebooks

Whether you choose a notebook or a desktop computer very much depends on what role you want IT to play in your business.

Desktop computers take up a significant amount of space and are designed to be set-up in a fixed location. On the upside, they are (generally) more comfortable to use for long periods of time than notebooks. You can also buy an equivalent desktop computer cheaper than a notebook, or if you wish, spend a little more and get a really powerful, fast desktop computer, although this is something you are only likely to need if you are frequently handling large image or audio files, or if you run many different applications at the same time. Desktop computers usually come in a 'tower' configuration, (which means they are higher than they are wide) and require a separate monitor, keyboard and mouse.

Notebook computers (sometimes called 'laptops', although health and safety guidelines advise against using them on your lap for prolonged periods of time) are generally more expensive than desktops of equivalent power. Their great advantage is mobility. You can take your notebook on the road with you quite easily, and use it to access the internet (via Wi-Fi or a G3 modem) in a huge variety of places, including cafés and pubs. Notebooks have integrated keyboards, monitors and mice or pointing devices, though you can use them with separate units connected by USB leads. If you are using your notebook in a fixed position, it is worth considering a laptop stand, which will position your screen at an ideal viewing height, helping to reduce neck strain. These range in price from £20 to £50 and many have built in USB connections for keyboard, mouse and printer. If you really must use it on your lap, you can buy 'laptop coasters', which are pads that sit between your body and the computer, greatly reducing the amount of radiated heat that your lower body has to absorb.

Of course, you may decide to acquire both a notebook and a desktop computer, depending on your needs. It is worth remembering that transferring data between your computers is a relatively simple affair, so if you want to run a desktop computer at home and a laptop for those times when you are away from the office, it is fairly easy to manage. Both systems can be set up on the same home network, or if you are working away, you can access data on your remote system via the internet using filehosting or remote access services such as www.gotomypc.com, or Apple's iDisk.

Operating Systems

There are a number of different operating systems (programs that govern a computer's behaviour and usability) on the market for home and business computer users. The market leaders are Microsoft Windows and Apple's Mac OS (which only runs on Apple computers). Each has its advantages and disadvantages.

On the grounds of price, the cheaper Windows may seem to be the natural choice for most business computer users, and it is the system that nearly everyone else in the business world uses. However, it would be unwise to write off Apple's

Windows vs. Mac

Microsoft Windows in its various forms, the most recent of which is Windows Vista, is the market leader among operating systems. It is used almost universally in business. Some of its disadvantages are related to its popularity. For example, all of the major computer viruses that have appeared since the information technology revolution began in the 1990s have been designed to attack Windows-based systems, although some of the security weaknesses that have traditionally affected versions of Windows have been explicitly addressed in the latest version of the system, Vista. The huge advantage of using Windows is that it represents a common technology across the business world, and runs all the major applications you are likely to need.

Mac OS, which only runs on Apple computers, is a growing force in the world of operating systems. For years, Mac OS has been popular with businesses working in the design and media sectors, although it has been slow to catch on with other businesses. This might be seen to be connected to the fact that the system only runs on Apple computers, which, like-for-like, are generally more expensive than the PCs that run Microsoft Windows. On the upside, Mac OS is felt by its users to be much more stable and reliable. In addition, more than 120,000 viruses have attacked computers running Windows since 1995. But during the same period there have been less than 170 known Mac viruses or malware, and virtually none that have done any serious damage to systems. In addition to the fact that virus developers know they will affect more computers if they aim at Windows, this could also be a reflection of the strength of Apple's security technology.

Mac OS, which has grown massively in popularity over the past few years and has a reputation as an operating system that offers stability, reliability and tight security.

Printers

Improvements in technology have brought prices tumbling over the last decade, and it is possible to buy a printer today for less than £30. It is worth remembering, however, that the manufacturers actually make their money on the ink cartridges. An apparently cheap printer will probably require expensive cartridges. If you plan on doing a lot of printing, check out the price of both the printer you are considering and the size and price of relevant ink cartridges.

When you are considering what type of printer to buy, think about your business and your home needs. If your business requirement is small, but you have a digital camera for personal use, you might benefit from a model that prints photographs as well as text. On the other hand, if your printer's primary purpose is to crank out standard A4 letters, it will work out more expensive in the long run to purchase a model that can also print photographs.

If you work in graphics, or if you frequently present detailed spreadsheets, an A3 printer may come in handy. In addition, if you are likely to be printing

> **《Manufacturers actually make their money on the ink cartridges. 》**

> **《You should try to make copies of your tax and VAT returns before you put them in the post. 》**

a lot of full colour work, it is more cost-effective to invest in a model that uses multiple colour cartridges rather than a combination colour cartridge.

Photocopiers, scanners and fax machines

Copies of paper documents can be very useful. In particular, you should try to make copies of your tax and VAT returns before you post them to HMRC. If you are querying an invoice or a delivery note, send a copy with your letter. If your telephone bill covers both personal and business calls, take a copy of the original and include it with your business expenses.

Most towns and cities have several copy shops that offer photocopying services for a few pence per sheet. In addition, many towns and even small villages have photocopying services within their local Post Offices and corner shops. Alternatively, you could buy a small, desktop photocopier for under £100.

If you are working with hard copy images, a high-resolution scanner is an absolute requirement. In addition, if your work involves copying original printed documents, a scanner used in conjunction with an OCR (optical character recognition) program will save you hours of typing. Many of today's scanners allow you to email pictures directly from the control panel, or automatically print a colour copy of an original print or document.

The rise of email has seen a reduction in the need for fax machines but, frustratingly, as some traditional businesses still use this technology as a main method of communication, you may still be asked to receive the odd fax. Rather than paying the local Post Office on average £1.50 a page for the privilege of receiving a fax, a handy alternative is to use a fax-to-email service which converts your faxes into an email which then lands in your inbox. This has the added benefit of being stored on your computer, which you can then forward to others or print out.

Before you go out and buy a separate printer, scanner, photocopier and a fax machine, consider the benefits of an all-in-one, or multi-function system. It can be much more cost-effective to purchase a single machine rather than three or four separate ones. An all-in-one printer/copier/fax will use less electricity to operate than several individual machines and will also take up much less space in your office. And, unless you require

heavy print runs, or photographic quality copies, the operating costs can also be lower with one machine as opposed to three or four.

RSI

Repetitive Strain Injury (RSI) is caused by work that involves repetitive movement, which in the case of home-based workers, usually means typing. Typing-based RSI usually manifests itself as pain or stiffness in the fingers or wrists, which is most often caused by:

- Hammering on the keys.
- Not taking sufficient work breaks.
- Poor seating positions.
- Overuse of a mouse.

> **"The rise of email has seen a reduction in the need for fax machines."**

Online fax to email options include www.efax.co.uk, www.fax.co.uk or www.businessclub365.com (which offers a free fax2email service as part of its membership's perks).

If you get a serious bout of RSI it can severely affect your ability to work, perhaps preventing you from using a computer altogether. There are a number of strategies you can use to defeat it. The most important of which is to take regular breaks. There are a number of applications you can download to remind you to take appropriate breaks: see www.rsiguard.com (for Windows) and www.publicspace.net/macbreakz (for Mac OS). Even a short 'microbreak' of twenty seconds every five minutes can, if interspersed with longer breaks throughout the day, make a huge difference.

Use a soft keyboard with a regular, smooth action. As keyboards age, individual keys can become stiff, leading to the build-up of RSIs as they are struck. Many RSI sufferers find notebook keyboards softer than standard desktop keyboards. On the other hand, some find that the flatter angle of notebook keyboards actually makes their condition worse. If you begin to suffer from RSI, try out a number of solutions and find out what works best for you.

Use a pointing device other than a mouse. Mice are relatively stressful to use. Consider instead using a pen tablet, which employs a flat surface (the tablet) and a pen (the pointing device) to direct the cursor on your computer screen.

Use alternative technologies, other than your keyboard, for getting words on to the screen. Dictation technology has improved dramatically in recent years, allowing you to dictate to your computer. It still is not perfect, but with a little training you can get excellent results. Windows Vista has speech recognition and dictation built in as standard. If you are using a pen tablet as a pointing device, you can also use handwriting recognition, whereby you actually use your own handwriting to enter data into your computer. Handwriting recognition currently comes as standard with Mac OS, which features the industry-leading Ink application for just this purpose.

TELEPHONES

Perhaps the most important must-have in any office is a telephone. Whilst mobiles are an accepted part of business communication, if you want to create the impression that you are more than a one-man business, a land line is a sound investment. If you are working from home, a separate business line reduces the chance of your children or partner picking up your business calls or being on the phone when an important caller is trying to contact you. If you are out the office consider diverting to your mobile or a telephone answering service. If you have to use an answer phone, take time out to record a personalised greeting rather than relying on the standard message.

❝ If you are working from home, a separate business line reduces the chance of your children or partner picking up your business calls or being on the phone when an important caller is trying to contact you. ❞

The telecommunications market is extremely competitive and there are plenty of opportunities to find a good deal. Your first step should be to work out your telephone habits. When do you use your phone most? Once you have done that, you can shop around for a tariff that gives you the cheapest calls during your personal peak-use hours.

Some telephone service providers combine landline and mobile phone packages. If your business requires you to spend a lot of time on the road, a cheap mobile service will help you keep business costs down. If your market is overseas, a package that offers cost-effective calls to your customer-base is far more preferable than one that offsets cheap weekend-calls in the UK by offering more expensive overseas calls.

If you work from home, a combined communications package that offers free or low cost digital television and broadband internet connection in addition to your landline may be a good cost effective option.

There are several websites, such as www.uswitch.com which will help you compare the prices and packages of several telephone operations and internet service providers. Spending a bit of time on research could help save your business several hundred pounds a year.

Voice over IP

A further money-saving option is to make use of Voice over IP (VoIP) technology. VoIP allows you to use some of your computer's bandwidth (roughly speaking, the volume of data that you can transmit

Jargon Buster

Voice over IP Voice over Internet Protocol is a technology that allows you to make telephone calls using the system of data transmission that drives the world wide web, email, and several other digital telecommunications technologies such as instant messaging.

to and receive from the internet at any one time) to make voice calls. Most companies offering VoIP charge for connection to the internet (including email and the internet) and not for individual calls. For this reason, VoIP can be extremely good value.

Systems currently available include Skype (www.skype.com) and VoIP Talk (www.voiptalk.org). At the time of writing VoIP technology is still relatively in its infancy, offering a worthwhile solution to businesses with good, fast internet connections. However, VoIP conversations can still be of variable quality and reliability when compared to a traditional landline, or even a mobile telephone conversation.

Where to get advice

When you become self-employed there will be no shortage of people offering you advice. Some of it will be excellent, some of it poor. But how do you tell the difference? And what are the best sources of advice when you are starting a new business?

Presenting your business to others

Before you seek advice or support, you need to think carefully about how to present your business idea. Devoting time and effort towards creating a presentation that works will pay rich dividends.

Presenting your business is simply a case of explaining your idea and your plans as clearly and persuasively as possible. It is a very useful, quick way of setting out your business to someone you wish to advise or support you.

Pitching is one of the first tests of any idea. How do you package your business plan to make it appeal to other people? The idea that seemed brilliant when you first thought of it can suddenly sound weak when you try to explain it to someone who does not share your passion or involvement.

In fact, this is one of the reasons why pitching is such an important exercise, it is a great way of exposing flaws and weaknesses in a business idea. It is very important to welcome feedback. Expect criticism and, when you get it, embrace it. It is better that you identify weaknesses early rather than have them trip you up when it is too late to change.

> ❝ Pitching is a great way of exposing flaws and weaknesses in a business idea. ❞

At the same time, be careful about outlining your plan before you understand it yourself. If you present a half-formed idea to anyone, whether it is your partner, your parents or your best friend, you are unlikely to get them to share your enthusiasm unless they themselves are very 'get up and go' people. At this stage you want constructive analysis, so develop your pitch fully and pick your listeners carefully.

The first stage of presenting your idea is to have a clear and precise sense of exactly what your business is going to do, where it is going to do it, who the target market will be and why that market needs your products or services. This is also the first stage of writing a business plan and conducting a SWOT analysis to identify Strengths, Weaknesses, Opportunities and Threats. We will cover planning and analysis in detail in the next chapter.

PRESENTATION

The best way to prepare for your presentation is by first breaking it down into bite-sized pieces. If you have a notebook, use a software application like

> **"** Encouraging feedback is a useful way of identifying strengths and weaknesses. **"**

Microsoft PowerPoint or Apple Keynote to take your audience through your concept. They can look at it on your notebook or, if one is available, you can project it on to a wall-mounted screen. Alternatively, use an A4 presenter which you can buy from a local stationer. Use images and simple diagrams to outline your plan. That way your audience can ask questions without causing you to lose track.

Many of your initial presentations may be in informal situations. Use them to practise for the real thing. If you demonstrate that you have thought your idea through and can capture it on a few sides of A4, you increase your chances of being taken seriously.

Case Study Sheena

Sheena plans to launch a small business that offers support to companies that are having temporary problems with their IT networks. Let us take a look at the way she answers our five questions:

What is your business going to do?
I have a strong background in IT and network management, so I'm going to offer a technical support and call-out service to small companies that are having network problems. I can deal with most cases remotely. If that isn't possible I will visit my customers' premises at no extra cost.

Who are the target customers?
There are lots of small businesses near where I live in Sheffield, that depend on their IT networks to track stock and manage staff and sales. They also don't usually have a dedicated member of staff to solve problems.

When do you intend to start?
I already have contacts offering me work, so if necessary I could start next week. However, before I start I want to secure funding to invest in a van, upgrade my own equipment, and design and distribute marketing materials. I've set a date of 1 October and I'm currently negotiating two contracts to start then.

Where will the business operate?
I'll base myself out of my own home. I've already converted my garage and have high-speed broadband access. There are a number of business parks in the Sheffield area where most of my customers will be based. I already have some contacts there who are interested in my services. I am also well placed for local transport connections.

How much competition is there?
There's competition from major network suppliers as well as independent computer retailers and specialists in town. However, my research suggests that much of the competition fails to deliver, because it hasn't built a strong understanding of the typical customer's real needs. As a result, demand for quality support outstrips the local supply.

Do not try to memorise your presentation word for word. Use the visuals as prompts and interact with your audience rather than just lecturing them. Each time you make a presentation you will improve, use this confidence to bond with your listeners. If you get a blank look when you make a point, ask if there are any questions. Encouraging feedback is a useful way of re-examining your own ideas. It will also help you to identify strengths and weaknesses you hadn't thought of previously.

Five easy steps

What	**is your business going to do?**
Who	**are the target customers?**
When	**do you intend to start?**
Where	**will the business operate?**
How	**much competition is there?**

When you are answering these questions, always try to think in terms of an identifiable market. Does the market exist, and is there a large enough gap in the existing supply for you to build a business?

When Sheena puts all her answers together, she has the basis for a good pitch. When you are thinking of yours, remember the way she approaches her market. Her pitch is concrete and precise, especially when it comes to defining her target customers. She does not talk vaguely about 'companies that need IT support'. Instead, she defines her customers as:

- Small businesses based in Sheffield.
- Dependent on their IT networks to track stock and manage staff and sales.
- Lacking a dedicated member of staff to solve problems.

The very first thing you should do before you even plan your business is identify your target market. Neglecting to do so is one of the main reasons businesses fail. If you cannot define your target market accurately in your pitch, you need to go back and think about your business idea afresh.

Jargon Buster

Pitch A pitch is any presentation where you try to sell your business idea. An example could be when you are presenting a business plan to a bank manager in a bid to raise capital to start your business. But the term also refers to presentations used to try and win work from other businesses. So an advertising agency, for instance, might have to pitch for most of the projects it wants to work on.

❝ Identifying your target market is the very first thing you should do. ❞

Responses to your pitch

It does not matter whom you make your pitch to, expect them to find problems with it. You might be surprised who is most critical. As we said in Chapter 1, there is a good chance that family and friends, who might be jealous or fearful, will do their best do discourage you.

On the other hand you might find someone else, whom you might expect to be more sceptical, is encouraging and accepts your vision.

Be wary of anyone who gives you an instant thumbs-up. Either you have confused them, they have not listened properly or they are not really interested. There is no business opportunity in the world that shouldn't prompt a few questions, and it is unlikely you will cover all the key points in your initial pitch.

When you get criticism, listen carefully and acknowledge it. 'Good question' is a positive response that also gives you to time think of an answer or ask for clarification. Respond positively with facts that support your approach. The key is to defend your pitch without getting defensive. Many of the questions you are asked, especially by a good business adviser, will be designed to make you think more deeply about your plans. If questioning identifies a genuine weakness, your questioner has done you a favour. You should then work with him or her to find a way of modifying your idea to deal with the problem.

66 Be wary of anyone who gives you an instant thumbs-up. Either you have confused them, they have not listened properly or they are not really interested. **99**

Who to ask for advice

Not everyone is a business expert, though plenty of people will have no hesitation in passing an opinion if they are asked, and even if they are not. It can be easy to become demoralised and confused when you get a hundred different opinions from a hundred different people.

Your best bet is to make a shortlist of people to ask. This should include people who really know what they're talking about, though you should also ask a couple of people who know you well. When you become self-employed, you become your business's key asset, and it's vital that you're aware of your own strengths and weaknesses as others see them.

Let's start with the source of advice that 29 per cent of all individuals who are thinking of becoming self-employed approach first; the bank.

Meeting your bank manager: some points to remember

- Listen to the manager's advice. He or she will have had many relationships with small business clients, and should have a good sense of what works and what does not.
- It is in the bank's interest that your business is successful. The small business adviser you see will probably have a good knowledge of local markets and, if he or she has been doing the job for a while, a good nose for assessing the viability of business plans.
- Business managers have a responsibility to their bank, it is in their interests to introduce you to products and services that their employers provide. It is for you to consider what is on offer and decide what you need.
- In the long term remember that when things go wrong it is the manager's job to do what is right for the bank rather than what is right for your business. With this in mind, it's worth considering the benefits of keeping your business and personal accounts with separate banks.
- On the other hand, remember bank employees are human like the rest of us. The overwhelming majority will genuinely wish you well, and may help you to grow your business by promoting it to their other customers.
- Bank business advisers will have had some training and experience in dealing with small business customers. However, it is very rare to find one that has actually 'been there and done it'. Training, no matter how good, is no substitute for direct experience of self-employment; remember that your bank adviser is unlikely to have had that experience.

Jargon Buster

Cashflow forecast An assessment of how cash is likely to flow through your business. **This is explained in greater detail in Chapter 10.**
Profit and loss forecast Similar to a cashflow forecast, but based on actual profits and losses rather than cash going in and out of your business.

None of these are as complicated as they sound, and we will discuss how to put them together in Chapter 5. Having them will make a big difference to how seriously your bank takes you, and more importantly, will increase your own understanding of what is required for you to achieve your goals. If your planning is sound and you can convince the bank that a market exists, having these documents should persuade the bank to look on you as a safe bet as a business borrower.

THE BANK

Banks see self-employed individuals and business start-ups as very important. Linking with a business at the start of its life is an ideal opportunity for a bank, and the more stable the background of the client, the more attractive the relationship. Take advantage of whatever free service your bank offers. If you have had a personal account with them for a while, it is likely that you have helped them to fund it! If you need start-up finance in the form of a loan or increased overdraft, a meeting with your bank's small business manager is an excellent starting point.

What your bank manager will want to see

If you are heading to see your bank manager, cap in hand, to seek finance as well as advice, you will need to take more than your business proposal or presentation. You should prepare:

- A business plan
- A cashflow forecast
- A profit and loss ("P&L") forecast

❝ Bank employees are human like the rest of us – the overwhelming majority will genuinely wish you well. ❞

AN ACCOUNTANT

An accountant, if you get the right one, is generally a good bet for independent advice. Accountants' advice is not free, but if you look around you should be able to find one who will give you a free initial consultation to discuss your business plans and you can take it from there.

Accountants, as you might expect, are most comfortable dealing with the finance. However, they often lean towards being more cautious in their outlook and may not be able to advise you on all aspects of your business.

FRIENDS AND FAMILY

We outlined the pitfalls of seeking advice from friends and family in Chapter 1. However, they do have a role to play, and you can hardly start a new venture without involving them at some stage. This is

65

Strengths and weaknesses of an accountant's business advice

Strengths	Weaknesses
Your accountant should be able to give you good advice about how to set up your business, decide on your pricing model, manage your cashflow, and correctly account for assets and liabilities.	Accountants tend to be cautious. Because they are frequently called in to rescue businesses in trouble they see the consequences of business failure more regularly than most people. Don't be surprised if your accountant focuses more on the problems your business faces rather than congratulating you on your proposal. Their job is to identify holes in your plan and that is exactly what a good accountant will do.
Your accountant will also be able to provide you with guidance on bookkeeping, take full advantage of legislation to maximise your tax position and assist you with completing your tax return.	By nature, accountants see businesses purely in terms of numbers. Again, this is hardly surprising, but it means you shouldn't expect your accountant to give expert advice on sales, marketing and human resources management.

especially true if you have children, or if your partner is taking responsibility for paying the mortgage and the bills while your business gets going. In these situations you'll probably want to get as much support as possible. Be definite about your research and your objectives, and focus on gaining their support. Do not expect immediate acceptance; give them time to think about it and understand the opportunity.

But as we said in the first chapter, it is difficult for them to be detached when asked for an objective view. Close family will want you to be successful but they need to balance the risks you are taking with the likelihood of success and the stress associated with self-employment.

Equally, close friends can have mixed emotions. As much as they may want you to succeed, they will not want to dent your

 To find a certified chartered accountant in your area, contact the Association of Chartered Certified Accountants or the Institute of Chartered Accountants. See useful addresses page 200 for further details.

enthusiasm or confidence, so in asking them for feedback, focus on questions that will give them an opportunity to make constructive criticism.

Do not discount the possibility that your friends may be a little envious. Quiet rivalries can exist in even the closest friendship. Do not get too suspicious of negative criticism, but bear this possibility in mind all the same.

OTHER SELF-EMPLOYED WORKERS

Without a doubt, some of the best people to talk to about self-employment are those that have actually done it. That does not just mean other people in your field, but anyone. Self-employed joiners and management consultants may fulfil very different roles, but they have in common a shared experience of working for themselves which they can pass on to you no matter what you do.

Try, if you can, to talk to a cross-section of people who work for themselves. One of the first things you will notice is that there are very few who have sailed effortlessly to the top of their trade. Most self-employed people have hit problems at one time or another. For the price of a couple of drinks, you can get a wealth of information and advice that your bank's business adviser or your accountant wouldn't be able to give you.

Approach a variety of successful self-employed workers and ask for some of their time. If you are serious, the majority will be more than happy to help, providing they have the time. After all, they have all been in exactly the same position you are in.

Questions to ask successful self-employed workers

- What is the toughest time you have had?
- What is the most important lesson you have learnt?
- How do you deal with banks, accountants and HMRC?
- What was the worst decision you have ever made and why?
- How do you manage to get the work/life balance right?

Ask open questions and learn from their 'real world' experience. You will probably find they share a variety of characteristics: confidence, skill at what they do and a capacity for hard work will be the most immediately obvious. One trait that might be less obvious, at least during an initial conversation, is a 'never say die' attitude. All businesses have tough times, especially in the first few years, and the ones that survive tend to be managed by individuals who have nerve and resilience.

Do not neglect those people for whom it has not worked out, either. Those who have failed at self-employment might do their best to put you off, either out of a sincere concern for your wellbeing or a dislike of seeing others succeed where they have not. Listen to their warnings, but pay more attention to working out why they failed. A good question to ask is 'what would they do differently if they had their time again?'

BUSINESS LINK

Business Link is the Government's official support network for small businesses in England. There are similar organisations in the rest of the UK – Business Eye in Wales, Invest Northern Ireland in Northern

67

Reasons why self-employment can fail

- Failing to focus on a specific target market.
- Not asking or listening to the customer.
- Failure to identify a need to change.
- Neglecting sales and marketing.
- Poor products, service or support.
- Not being prepared to do what it takes to succeed.

Ireland, and Business Gateway and Highlands and Islands Enterprise in Scotland. For the purposes of this section, we'll use 'Business Link' as a catch-all term.

Business Link is ultimately funded by the Department for Business, Enterprise and Regulatory Reform (formerly the DTI) supported by a number of other government departments, agencies and local authorities. The nine individual Business Links are managed by Regional Development Agencies (RDAs).

When you are first starting out, Business Link can be a very useful source of advice. Its main role is that of a broker. Rather than providing all the advice and help itself, it fast-tracks customers to the expert help they need. When you contact a Business Link office you will probably be invited in for an interview. If you find this useful and you want to go further down the route of government-funded assistance, a meeting will be arranged with a local Enterprise Agency (see opposite) – one of the independent organisations that hold government contracts to deliver support to new and small businesses.

Business Links can be very useful sources of information about local opportunities. However, as with banks and some other sources of advice, it is useful to remember that Business Link staff members do not necessarily have personal experience of self-employment.

Jargon Buster

SME Small to medium-sized enterprise, typically numbering 1-250 employees.

ENTERPRISE AGENCIES

Enterprise Agencies can take a number of forms. They are not government agencies, but independent organisations committed to respond to the needs of small and growing businesses. In particular they target pre-start, start-up and micro businesses (1-10 employees) helping them to achieve their objectives, and encouraging growth and stability.

If you approach a Business Link (or one of the Scottish, Northern Irish or Welsh equivalents) the chances are you will wind up being referred to a local Enterprise Agency. You will be assigned a business adviser to guide you as your launch your business.

Enterprise Agency staff are very useful, not only for their business expertise, but because they have a wide knowledge of the grants and opportunities available for small businesses.

What to expect

Unlike the advice you get from your bank manager, support and guidance

United Kingdom

Shell LiveWire – a worldwide organisation for young entrepreneurs aged 16-30.
www.shell-livewire.com

The Department for Business, Enterprise and Regulatory Reform – has a useful section of its website dedicated to small business.
www.dberr.gov.uk

The Fredericks Foundation – focuses on giving advice and support to "...the financially disadvantaged, unemployed, single parents, ex-offenders and disabled people of any age".
www.fredericksfoundation.org

BusinessClub365 – offers advice and a range of special offers to new and growing businesses.
www.businessclub365.com

Smallbusiness.co.uk – is a comprehensive web portal offering advice on all aspects of starting and running a small business.
www.smallbusiness.co.uk

The Institute of Business Consulting – offers business advice and mentoring.
www.ibconsulting.org.uk

Small Firms Enterprise Development Initiative (SFEDI) – Provides a range of support services for small businesses.
www.sfedi.co.uk

England

Business Link – business support and advice for start-ups and SMEs.
www.businesslink.gov.uk 0845 600 9006

Scotland

Business Gateway – business support and advice for new and growing businesses in Scotland.
www.bgateway.com 0845 609 6611

Highlands and Islands Enterprise – business and community support and advice in the Highlands and Islands of Scotland.
www.hie.co.uk

Wales

Business Eye – free and impartial advice for businesses in Wales.
www.businesseye.org.uk 08457 96 97 98

Llygad Busnes/Business Eye – free and impartial advice for businesses in Wales.
www.businesseye.org.uk 08457 96 97 98

Northern Ireland

Invest Northern Ireland – support for start-ups, existing businesses and businesses looking to relocate to Northern Ireland.
www.investni.com

---

from Enterprise Agencies are generally delivered by business advisers who have direct experience of running a business.

Enterprise Agencies secure their funding from various sources including Local Authority, Central Government and Europe. The exact services available will depend on the contract they are delivering, but in all cases you are generally assigned a business adviser who will work with you to develop your plan and start your business.

Your Enterprise Agency business adviser will also help you find other expert advice, which will be useful if you are working in a specialist area such as technology. Depending on your specific location you may also be able to access grants and business loans. Funds are more likely to be available in deprived areas, but in every instance it is worth checking with your business adviser just in case something is available.

It is extremely important to build a rapport with your business adviser. Your work with him or her is a two-way relationship: the more effort and determination you put in the greater the response and support you will receive. Business advisers are motivated by helping others achieve success. Make sure you give them their pay-off by involving them and acknowledging their ideas. At the same time, remember that ultimately it is down to you to make everything work.

THE PRINCE'S TRUST

The Prince's Trust helps young people aged 18-31 to get started in business. It can provide guidance, mentoring and interest-free loans or grants to help young people start in business.

If you are unemployed, the Trust can also help you access:

- A low interest loan of up to £4,000 for a sole trader, or up to £5,000 for a partnership (the average loan is between £2,000 and £3,000 but varies regionally).
- A grant of up to £1,500 in special circumstances (subject to local availability).
- A test marketing grant of up to £250.
- On-going advice from a volunteer business mentor.

PRIME

If you are no longer a spring chicken, don't worry because at the other end of the age group spectrum you can get support from PRIME. PRIME is specifically geared to help people over the age of 50 set up in business. It is a registered charity linked to Age Concern England and was founded by the Prince of Wales, who remains PRIME's President. PRIME is a member of the Prince's Charities Group. PRIME offers a sympathetic ear, free information and help, workshops and business networking events. PRIME can also refer you to properly-accredited advisers in partner organisations for free business advice, and provide help and advice on starting a social enterprise.

 In April 2007 the Institute of Business Advisers merged with the Institute of Management Consultancy to become the Institute of Business Consulting.

 For the Prince's Trust, see www.princes-trust.org.uk or call 0800 842 842. For the Prince's Scottish Youth Business Trust, see www.psybt.org.uk or call 0141 248 4999. For PRIME see www.primeinitiative.org.uk or call 0800 783 1904.

Planning for success

When you are full of enthusiasm for a new business it can be very tempting to start right away. However, you are much more likely to succeed if you do some planning first. And if you need to raise finance, a business plan is essential.

What's the point of a plan?

Launching a business without a plan is like acting in a play that does not have a script. Working for yourself is hard enough without having to do your planning on the hoof. In this section we are going to look at the benefits that a formal business plan offers, and the approaches you might take in developing your own.

A quick search of the web will reveal dozens of different templates and software applications for developing a business plan. However, do not let the complexity of what is on offer daunt you. The essence of good planning is clarity and simplicity.

It is important to draw a distinction between the plan and the planning. The plan is the document you end up with; the piece of paper that outlines your objectives and how you are going to achieve them. The planning is, in some ways, more important than the plan. It is a process that forces you to actually think about the business you are intending to start. No matter how confident you are about any aspect of your business, you can't get away with writing 'I've got that covered' on a plan.

Even if you do not need to raise finance, a formal plan will give your business a definite starting point as well as a benchmark against which to judge future progress.

STRUCTURE

Business plans tend to follow a set, though flexible, format. Because you are a self-employed individual starting a small operation, your bank will not really expect you to write the detailed and highly-structured document that a large business would produce. However, it is a good idea to know what kind of standards of planning are expected of larger businesses. You can learn from their approach and adapt their planning models to suit your own ends.

Any business plan you write, whether it is designed to convince a lender, or simply to help clarify your own ideas, does not need to be very long. Entrepreneurs putting together a large or complex business may end up writing a plan that is dozens of pages in length. However, if you are running a small business, and

Purpose of a formal business plan

- To express in concrete terms the aims and methods of your business.
- To prepare financial projections that demonstrate the business is viable and justifies the investment of time, money and resources.
- To establish to third parties (lenders, partners, accountants) that you have fully thought through the business opportunity and have a clear strategy for exploiting it.

particularly if you are a sole trader with no employees, your plan may only contain a single page, or less, for each of the major sections.

Business plan structure*

1. **Summary.**
2. **Background information.**
3. **The product or service.**
4. **Marketing.**
5. **Day-to-day running (sometimes known as the 'operating plan').**
6. **Financial needs and projections.**
7. **A risk-assessment (usually in the form of a SWOT analysis – see the end of this chapter).**

---

*Each part of this seven-point structure is outlined in greater detail in both the sub-sections and case studies of this chapter.

1. SUMMARY

In some business plans this is known as the 'executive summary'. The idea of this section is simple: to present the basic outline of your business. Unless you are starting a relatively large or complex business, this may be just one or two paragraphs, so that somebody who picks up your plan and just glances at it can get a good idea of your business proposition on the very first page.

Ideally, it should sum up everything that comes afterwards, explaining what product or service you plan to sell, whom you are planning to sell it to, your long-term goals and any start-up finance required. If your new business is fairly standard, and requires little or no funding, it is likely that your summary will be less than 100 words

long. If you are struggling to summarise your business within those constraints, it is possible that you need to look at your basic idea again. Is it over-complex, or dependent on too many factors beyond your control?

It is important to be positive. Words like 'if', 'maybe' and 'hopefully', don't inspire confidence and suggest that you have not thought the idea through. Rather than say 'we hope our turnover will be £50,000', use 'we forecast a £50,000 turnover'. Instead of 'we will try to do business on the internet', use 'we will use the internet to promote our business'. The fact is you are writing about the future; if you are not definate about it, your readers will not believe it is going to happen. If your basic idea is not as watertight as you thought, you will need to revisit it.

Sales tool

If you are intending to use a formal business plan to help raise money, bear in mind that you are using it, in effect, as a sales tool – a document designed to convince its readers that your business is worth backing. Your business plan is a structured document that 'sells' its readers the idea that your business is likely to succeed. So before you write your plan you might find it useful to absorb the lessons of Chapter 7, Sales and Marketing.

When you actually produce the plan, make sure it is a smart, well-presented document written in plain, clear, accurate English. A tatty plan full of misspellings is not going to make a good impression.

Annie is 35. Since graduating from university, she has worked as a footwear buyer and has gained experience working for specialist high street chains. She is now planning to quit her job and become a self-employed sales consultant, working from home. She requires a computer, some office equipment and some cash to cover international travel expenses. She has decided to approach her bank for start-up finance to cover these costs, and is writing a business plan on which to base her request for a loan.

After some thought, Annie writes the first paragraph of her summary:

66 Under the trading name Annie Wong and Associates, I will provide advice and consultancy services to manufacturers of high quality footwear that wish to sell their products to retail outlets in the UK. Specifically I will use my specialist knowledge and design skills to assist manufacturers and my contacts within the retail industry to deal directly with potential buyers on their behalf. 99

This is a fair summary. Notice, though, that Annie has still been a bit vague about her target market. Her description,

'manufacturers of high quality footwear that wish to sell their products to retailer outlets', encompasses a broad range of business opportunities. She could still tighten her definition and, for example, target manufacturers of high quality ladies' footwear that are based in the Far East and seeking to sell their products to designer footwear chains in the UK.

She has the chance to describe her target customers in the fourth part of her business plan (marketing), but even at this stage it is useful to be as precise as possible about target markets.

2. BACKGROUND

All business is fundamentally about people. If you are planning to become a self-employed sole trader, the 'background' section will be about just one person, you. In it, you will need to explain who you are, what you have done in the past and what skills and expertise you will be bringing to your business.

If you are launching a partnership or a limited company with employees or co-directors who are a fundamental part of the enterprise, or essential to the success of the business, you should include them too.

For Annie, preparing the background section was relatively straightforward. If you find yours more difficult to write, you will need to look again at your own skills and experience, and define how well they will fit into the kind of business you are trying to launch.

The sort of self-analysis that writing a formal plan requires you to perform, makes the whole exercise worth it for its own sake, irrespective of whether you are intending to present the plan to a lender or not.

3. PRODUCTS & SERVICES

In the products and services section of your business plan, you need to outline what it is that you are actually going to supply to your customers. Rather than just listing standard products and services,

Case Study 2 — Annie

The background section is an important part of Annie's plan, because her potential for success is based on the experience and contacts she has gained in her previous employment. She writes:

66 The growing influence, competitive pricing and the increasing quality of materials and workmanship is allowing Chinese industry to move from mass markets towards fulfilling niche demands. If Chinese shoe manufacturers are to penetrate the UK specialist market, they need to change the attitudes of British footwear buyers and their customers' perceptions. Although I was born and brought up in the UK, my family is Chinese. I have always had an interest in the language and culture of China. I graduated from London University's School of Oriental and African Studies with a First Class degree in East Asian Languages in 1993. My course included a year in China and Hong Kong, developing my skills in Mandarin and Cantonese.

I have always been interested in fashion. Following university, I decided upon a career in retail buying. Over the course of a 14-year career I worked as a buyer for Bally, Kurt Geiger and Pied à Terre before moving to become Senior Buyer at House of Fraser. As well as making dozens of contacts I developed an understanding of range planning and the needs of specialist stores. I believe my knowledge, experience and contacts will be vital to the success of my new venture. 99

give the details of your specific offering. Explain how it will fit into the gaps in the market. Identify areas where your offering could develop or grow. What exactly would your target customers want if you could deliver it? What frustrates them about current suppliers?

Very few businesses are lucky enough to exist without any competition. Any viable business plan must offer an outline of the competition and include a strategy for dealing with it. That would normally include a discussion of your business's Unique Selling Proposition (USP). The USP represents the benefits you can provide to your customers that few, or even none of your competitors, offer. This may be speedy delivery or an after-sales service, for example. A very common

USP is value, but it is important not to confuse value with price. Although the price of your product or service is very important, if it is your only selling point you should be prepared for a tough future. There will always be somebody who will be prepared to undercut you, and trading at the bottom end of any market leaves no room for investment. In addition, it is possible to pitch your offer too cheaply: customers are well aware that they tend to get what they

66 Any viable business plan must offer an outline of the competition and include a strategy for dealing with it. 99

Case Study 3   Annie

For Annie this is her opportunity to outline why she is different.

❝ I am fluent in Mandarin, Cantonese and English and have a comprehensive knowledge of the needs of the UK market. I will work with high quality Chinese manufacturers to help them create the right product offer and marketing materials. Working on their behalf I will build relationships with targeted UK footwear buyers to create a product range that works supported by prices and delivery schedules to match their needs. I can work on a standard agency basis or as a retained consultant with an incentive package. ❞

pay for. They may be suspicious of a deal that seems too good to be true.

Writing a formal business plan will help you to concentrate on the true nature of the competition your enterprise will face and develop precise strategies for dealing with it.

Types of USP to help your business

- Offer an all-inclusive package or service that removes all possible hassles for the customer.
- Make a difference and do what other suppliers in your market fail to do.
- Encourage repeat business with customer loyalty rewards or a low-cost offer.
- Exploit your location or method of delivery by doing business in an area or route to market that is ignored or under-serviced by your competitors.
- Identify a very specific target or niche market and develop a product or service that is exactly right for it.

4. MARKETING

The term 'marketing' should not be confused with 'advertising', though in business circles you will often hear the words used as if they mean the same thing. A good definition of marketing is: the process of identifying a market for your product, defining its need and communicating with it. In other words, marketing is not just about selling your wares. It's about working out who's going to want to buy them and how you're going to connect with these potential customers. Throughout the preceding chapters we have tried to hammer home the importance of catering for a tightly defined target market. So in this part of your plan you need to identify:

- Your target market(s).
- How you intend to reach them (your 'route to market').

Be as precise as possible. If you already have customers lined up, name them. If you do not, give examples of typical customers in your chosen market. If you are selling primarily to other businesses (a 'business to business' or 'b2b' operation), you can even give specific examples of the firms you are targeting. If, on the other hand, your customers will be members of the public ('consumers') it is useful to profile them using demographic and geographic information. So, for example, if you were customising and repairing skateboards you might say that your target market was the skater sub-culture, which predominantly consists of males aged 13-19, within a specific distance of your base.

Case Study 4   Annie

For Annie, the marketing section defines her focus. There is such a wide diversity of potential customers that she needs to make sure she doesn't become too vague. Also, because many of them are based overseas, she has to be careful about defining her route to market.

How will she advertise her services to Chinese companies, for example?

66 My primary target market will be high-quality manufacturers seeking to break into the UK footwear market. Typically these are medium-sized firms of 10-100 employees based in the cities of eastern China, principally Shanghai and Hong Kong. Examples include Jackie Woo and John Masouri.

I have two main strategies for marketing my services to these companies:

- I already have a number of contacts in the key manufacturing areas I have identified. One of my first priorities will be to expand this network. Many companies in China are still quite traditional in the way they do business, so I will travel to Shanghai and Hong Kong to meet important new contacts in person. Although telephone lines to China aren't always great, I can also use my fluent Chinese language skills to build rapport with potential clients over the telephone.

- I plan to establish an English/Chinese website to promote my services. An increasing number of Chinese companies are becoming aware of the possibilities the internet offers, and I intend to raise my profile in China by working with a freelance journalist who is very interested in my story. I will also run free seminars on exporting to the UK though an exhibition contact I have in Shanghai. 99

5. DAY-TO-DAY RUNNING

For some businesses, particularly those with large turnovers or an involved production or service process, the operational section of a business plan can be the most complex. For most self-employed workers, it is much simpler.

- If you are going to be working from home it might be a good idea to outline how you plan to strike a balance between your business and your personal life. Your bank manager will know that problems with life balance are some of the biggest hurdles the self-employed must overcome, with potential consequences for the long-term futures of their businesses. He or she will want to see that you have made plans to deal with work/life conflicts on a daily basis.

Jargon Buster

Demographics A method of defining target markets and groups of people in terms of age, income, location, personal interests and other factors. You can use this information to identify a 'target demographic' for your business.

Case Study 5 Annie

For Annie, there is a good chance that managing the day-to-day running of her business will become one of the biggest problems she faces. When she is planning her business, she cannot leave her personal life out of the equation, especially since that personal life includes looking after two small children. When she was in full-time work, childcare was expensive. It has become less expensive since they both started primary school.

However, the provision of childcare in itself is not the major problem. Annie's husband, Matt, works nights and is home in time to do the school run. The difficulty is going to be that Annie will have to work irregular hours and sometimes be away from home for long periods at a stretch; not the ideal situation for raising a family.

In her business plan she recognises this as a potential problem.

❝ Integrating my business with my family life is going to cause two specific problems:

- I will often have to work unsociable hours, including getting up very early in the morning to handle the time difference between the UK and China.
- I anticipate spending around ten per cent of my time, five weeks a year, in China. This will put additional pressure on my husband. However, my mother-in-law is very supportive and lives nearby. She has promised to help.

Although these problems cannot be avoided altogether, I believe they can be relieved by two key strategies:

- Managing my time carefully. The upside of doing a lot of work with China is that I may be able to take some regular time out in the late afternoon and early evening to spend with my children. This will not always be possible, because my role involves dealing with UK companies too. However, I think setting aside family time every day is vital.
- Using the internet for communications. I intend to use my website and email to minimise the time I spend either in China or on the phone to Chinese companies. However, I also recognise that Chinese business culture still places a great deal of emphasis on telephone communication and face-to-face dealings. ❞

Working through her business plan has helped Annie get a clear sense of some of the problems she might face, as well as potential solutions to them.

6. FINANCIAL NEEDS AND PROJECTIONS

An essential part of any business plan is an assessment of finance. That includes:

- The amount of start-up finance required.
- Cashflow forecast for the first 12 months.
- Profit and loss forecast for first three years' trading.
- Assumptions made on any of the above.

Planning for success

Case Study 6 Annie

Annie's list of start-up costs is fairly straightforward. It includes all the equipment she needs for her office and the expenses incurred while travelling abroad. She also includes the cost of setting up her website, creating marketing materials and her wages for the first three months. Although she has put money by to cover this, it is important to account for it in the plan. This will also need to be taken into account when she is dealing with her first tax return.

Annie's estimated start-up costs

Monthly costs	Monthly expenses	Cash needed to start	One-time costs	Cash needed to start
Salary (3 months)	£1,500	£4,500	Fixtures and equipment	£1,000
Travel	-	£1,500	Decoration and refurbishment	-
Rent	-	-	Website	£1,000
Advertising	-	-	Starting stock inventory	-
Delivery expenses	-	-	Marketing materials	£600
Supplies/			Legal and other professional fees	£250
Office stationery	£100	£300	Licences and permits	-
Telephone	£100	£300	Advertising and promotion	
Other utilities	-	-	for opening	£150
Insurance	-	-	Cash	-
NIC	£26	£26	Computer equipment	£1,000
Interest on loans	-	-	**Subtotal**	**£4,000**
Maintenance	-	-		
Legal and other				
professional fees	-	-		
Miscellaneous	-	-		
Subtotal		**£6,626**	**Total estimated start-up capital**	**£10,626**

Annie's cashflow projection (*Assumptions page 83)

	April	May	June	July	August
Carried forward	£0	£6,341	£3,272	£953	£729
Receipts					
Retained contracts	-	-	-	£1,250	£1,250
Other services	-	-	£250	£250	£250
Bank loan	£3,500	-	-	-	-
Cash injection	£6,500	-	-	-	-
Total receipts	**£10,000**	**£0**	**£250**	**£1,500**	**£1,500**
Total cash available	**£10,000**	**£6,341**	**£3,522**	**£2,453**	**£2,229**
Costs					
Wages	-	-	-	-	-
Travel	£500	£500	£500	£500	£500
Rent	-	-	-	-	-
Advertising	£75	£75	-	-	-
Marketing material	£250	£200	£150	-	-
Website	£250	£500	£250	£15	£15
Telephone	£100	£100	£100	£100	£100
Office stationery	£100	£100	£100	£40	£40
Utilities	£25	£25	-	-	-
Legal & professional	£250	-	-	-	-
Other expenses	-	-	-	-	-
Annie's drawings	£1,000	£1,000	£1,000	£1,000	£1,000
National Insurance	£9	£9	£9	£9	£9
Loan payment	-	£60	£60	£60	£60
Capital purchases					
General start-up costs	-	-	-	-	-
Computer equipment	£500	£250	£250	-	-
Fixtures & fittings	£600	£250	£150	-	-
Total costs	**£3,659**	**£3,069**	**£2,569**	**£1,724**	**£1,724**
Cash balance	**£6,341**	**£3,272**	**£953**	**£729**	**£505**

September	October	November	December	January	February	March
£505	£606	£882	£1,158	£1,434	£1,710	£1,986
£1,500	£1,500	£1,500	£1,500	£1,500	£1,500	£1,500
£500	£500	£500	£500	£500	£500	£500
-	-	-	-	-	-	-
-	-	-	-	-	-	-
£2,000	**£2,000**	**£2,000**	**£2,000**	**£2,000**	**£2,000**	**£2,000**
£2,505	£2,606	£2,882	£3,158	£3,434	£3,710	£3,986
-	-	-	-	-	-	-
£500	£500	£500	£500	£500	£500	£500
-	-	-	-	-	-	-
£175	-	-	-	-	-	-
-	-	-	-	-	-	-
£15	£15	£15	£15	£15	£15	£15
£100	£100	£100	£100	£100	£100	£100
£40	£40	£40	£40	£40	£40	£40
-	-	-	-	-	-	-
-	-	-	-	-	-	-
£1,000	£1,000	£1,000	£1,000	£1,000	£1,000	£1,000
£9	£9	£9	£9	£9	£9	£9
£60	£60	£60	£60	£60	£60	£60
-	-	-	-	-	-	-
-	-	-	-	-	-	-
-	-	-	-	-	-	-
£1,899	£1,724	£1,724	£1,724	£1,724	£1,724	£1,724
£606	£882	£1,158	£1,434	£1,710	£1,986	£2,262

Annie's profit and loss forecast**

	April	May	June	July	August	September
Income						
Retained contracts	-	-	£1,250	£1,250	£1,500	£1,500
Other services	-	£250	£250	£250	£500	£500
Total income	-	**£250**	**£1,500**	**£1,500**	**£2,000**	**£2,000**
Costs						
Annie's drawings	£1,000	£1,000	£1,000	£1,000	£1,000	£1,000
National Insurance	£9	£9	£9	£9	£9	£9
Travel	£500	£500	£500	£500	£500	£500
Rent	-	-	-	-	-	-
Advertising	£75	£75	-	-	-	£175
Marketing material	£250	£200	£150	-	-	-
Website	£250	£500	£250	£15	£15	£15
Telephone	£100	£100	£100	£100	£100	£100
Office stationery	£100	£100	£100	£40	£40	£40
Utilities	£25	£25	£25	£25	£25	£25
Legal & professional	£250	-	-	-	-	-
Finance interest	£36	£36	£36	£36	£36	£36
Depreciation	£25	£25	£39	£46	£46	£46
Other expenses	-	-	-	-	-	-
Total costs	**£2,620**	**£2,570**	**£2,209**	**£1,771**	**£1,771**	**£1,946**
Profit/loss	**-£2,620**	**-£2,320**	**-£709**	**-£271**	**£229**	**£54**
Cumulative profit/loss	**-£2,620**	**-£4,940**	**-£5,649**	**-£5,920**	**-£5,691**	**-£5,637**

PROFIT AND LOSS FORECAST

This is the profit and loss (P&L) forecast that Annie prepares for her business. Although at first glance a P&L may seem complicated, it is actually straightforward and logical. Your business adviser or accountant should be able to help you set one up. In addition, there are free templates available on the internet or from your bank that you can use as a base.

As Annie's business doesn't involve buying and selling or creating a product, she doesn't calculate a gross profit. An example P&L for this type of business is shown on page 84.

October	November	December	January	February	March	Total year 1
£1,500	£1,500	£1,500	£1,500	£1,500	£1,500	£14,500
£500	£500	£500	£500	£500	£500	£4,750
£2,000	£2,000	£2,000	£2,000	£2,000	£2,000	£19,250
£1,000	£1,000	£1,000	£1,000	£1,000	£1,000	£12,000
£9	£9	£9	£9	£9	£9	£108
£500	£500	£500	£500	£500	£500	£6,000
-	-	-	-	-	-	-
-	-	-	-	-	-	£325
-	-	-	-	-	-	£600
£15	£15	£15	£15	£15	£15	£1,135
£100	£100	£100	£100	£100	£100	£1,200
£40	£40	£40	£40	£40	£40	£660
£25	£25	£25	£25	£25	£25	£300
-	-	-	-	-	-	£250
£36	£36	£36	£36	£36	£36	£432
£46	£46	£46	£46	£46	£46	£503
-	-	-	-	-	-	-
£1,771	£1,771	£1,771	£1,771	£1,771	£1,771	£23,513
£229	£229	£229	£229	£229	£229	-£4,263
-£5,408	-£5,179	-£4,950	-£4,721	-£4,492	-£4,263	-£4,263

* Annie's cashflow assumptions
- All purchases paid for in the same month as invoice is received.
- All sales invoices paid in 30 days.
- One retained contract secured in year one.
- 'Other services' relate to consultancy and sales commissions.

**Annie's P&L assumptions
- Fixtures and fittings depreciated over 5 years.
- Computer Equipment depreciated over 3 years.
- For loan payments, interest only is included on P&L.
- This business is non-VAT rated, therefore all costs include VAT.

Notes: On the strength of her cashflow and P&L Annie's bank agrees to a £1,000 overdraft facility.

Example P&L for a business selling products

Sales		**£7,500**
Opening stock	-	-
Product costs	£15,000	-
Labour costs	£2,000	-
Total	**£17,000**	-
Less closing stock	£13,500	-
Cost of sales	**£3,500**	**-£3,500**
Gross profit		**£4,000**
Other costs		
Wages	£1,000	-
National Insurance	£9	-
Travel	£500	-
Rent	-	-
Advertising	£75	-
Marketing material	£250	-
Website	£250	-
Telephone	£100	-
Office stationery	£100	-
Utilities	£25	-
Legal & professional	£250	-
Finance interest	£36	-
Depreciation	£25	-
Total costs	**£2,620**	**-£2,620**
Net profit		**£1,380**

Annie's 3 year P&L projections

TOTAL	Year 1	Year 2	Year 3
Income			
Retained contracts	£14,500	£16,500	£19,500
Other services	£4,750	£8,500	£1,600
Total receipts	**£19,250**	**£25,000**	**£35,500**
Costs			
Annie's drawings	£12,000	£12,000	£12,000
National Insurance	£108	£108	£108
Travel	£6,000	£8,000	£10,000
Rent	-	-	-
Advertising	£325	£500	£750
Marketing material	£600	£300	£300
Website	£1,135	£600	£600
Telephone	£1,200	£1,350	£1,500
Office stationery	£660	£480	£480
Utilities	£300	£300	£300
Legal & professional	£250	£200	£200
Finance interest	£432	£432	£432
Depreciation	£503	£552	£552
Other expenses	-	-	-
Total costs	**£23,513**	**£24,822**	**£27,222**
Profit/loss	**-£4,263**	**£178**	**£8,278**
Cumulative profit/loss	**-£4,263**	**-£4,085**	**£4,193**

7. ASSESSMENT OF RISK

Do not fall into the trap of thinking that assessing risks just means keeping an eye on the competition. There are other threats that businesses face, too. We have already dealt with the personal problems that can arise from self-employment. It is also important to recognise that some threats are beyond your control. Markets may change very quickly, and if your business is to survive you must be prepared to change with them.

For example, a self-employed insurance broker launching a business in 1990 might be forgiven for thinking that he had a job for life. Surely people would always need insurance? However, he would not have been able to foresee the rise of the internet and the effect it would have reducing the role of the middle man from the domestic insurance market.

Case Study 7   Annie

Annie is well aware that she is not the only sales consultant who has seen the potential of Far Eastern markets. There are already a number of consultants who specialise in advising Chinese manufacturers on dealing with UK buyers.

❝ My two major competitors are Jennie Page and Patrick Jenson. Both are established agents and have good reputations within the buying community.

However, I have two key advantages: although they have wide experience and an excellent knowledge of the UK retail market, they do not exclusively operate in my niche area and neither can speak both of the two main eastern Chinese languages. They work in English with English-speaking Chinese clients or rely on translators. I believe my language skills will enable me to form relationships with clients very quickly, and my buying contacts in the top end of the UK footwear market will give me an edge that is difficult to compete with. ❞

Annie sees technology as a threat, too, and one she should keep an eye on.

❝ In the future technology may produce more advanced translation software, allowing my competitors to communicate with Chinese customers more effectively. However, in commercial buying, one-to-one relationships are key and that is the advantage I have.

An expansion of the online trade marketplace could also be a threat. Foreign wholesalers are already using trade directory sites to deal direct with western buyers. However, I see this as an opportunity. I can use the internet to advertise my services directly to interested parties on the relevant sites. ❞

85

SWOTTING UP

A one-page document that sums up your offer is very useful. A SWOT (Strengths, Weaknesses, Opportunities and Threats) analysis forces you to consider all the main elements and write them down in a simple table.

- **Strengths.** What strengths do I have that will help me to achieve my objective? How can I use or exploit these Strengths?
- **Weaknesses.** What weaknesses do I have that could prevent me from succeeding? How can I reduce or remove these Weaknesses?
- **Opportunities.** What external factors exist that will help me achieve my objectives? How can I exploit and take advantage of these Opportunities?
- **Threats.** What external factors or conditions could prevent me from succeeding? How can I defend or minimise these Threats?

Annie's SWOT analysis

Annie creates her SWOT analysis as a table. It is short, which is exactly how it should be. The reader needs to be able to see the business in simple terms.

Internal	Strengths	Weaknesses
	• Reputation as a top buyer.	• Never been self-employed.
	• Native Chinese multilingual.	• No agency track record.
	• Established relationships with manufacturers and other retail buyers.	• Little start-up capital.
	• Design skills and knowledge of UK market.	
	• Understanding of challenges facing manufacturers and buyers.	
External	**Opportunities**	**Threats**
	• China – increasing profile for quality and price.	• Established agents could increase focus on niche designer areas.
	• International currency increases attraction: strong £ versus $.	• Increased use of internet for establishing trading connections.
	• Target manufacturers and buyers using internet offering negotiation and consultancy service.	

Finance

So you have created your vision and developed your plan. You must now establish exactly how much money you need to get your business up and running. Before you can start thinking about how to raise the finance, it is important to get a clear sense of exactly what you require and how much this is likely to cost.

How much do you really need?

It is very important to plan thoroughly and take everything into account, when tackling the subject of money. There is nothing more frustrating than successfully raising finance and then discovering two months into your business that you do not have all the funds you need.

It is very easy to underestimate the costs involved in working for yourself. You have probably thought about your major expenses, such as: computer equipment, advertising and marketing, and other important items. But it is often the smaller items that that get overlooked and cause a shortfall. Minor expenses not accounted for like insurance, postage, stationery, travel and telephone bills can soon add up to significant sums of money.

For the purposes of planning, the finance you will require can generally be split into two parts. First, you must consider how much you will need to set up the business. This is known as your 'start-up capital'. After you have worked that out, you need to think about how much you need to run the business before you expect to generate enough cashflow for it to pay for itself. This is called 'working capital'.

START-UP CAPITAL

This should cover all your initial set-up costs, the one-off investments you need to start trading. This includes setting up your office, workshop or whatever everyday working environment you need. That may mean buying computers, tools, software packages and any kind of specialist professional equipment you need to run your business. Your set-up costs should also include cash for your initial marketing budget, your launch campaign and legal and professional costs.

What do you actually need?

As well as having a clear sense of exactly how much you need to start your venture, it is important to carefully manage the money you have available. You would probably think twice about being careless with funds of your own, so treat money

Planning point

It is very easy to spend money, particularly when it is not yours, so it is a good idea to treat money you have received from loans and investors as if it is your own hard-earned cash.

you have borrowed with the same respect. You will, after all, have to pay it all back (with interest) eventually.

Because of the importance of spending wisely, it is a good idea to separate those investments that are vital from those that can wait until your business is a bit more established. Train yourself from the outset to get value from every part of your budget and consider your needs carefully.

You may like the idea of driving around in a brand-new, leased BMW, but do you really need it? If it is a case of simply wanting a nice car rather than needing one, you are far more likely to appreciate it, (and far more likely to be able to bear the cost), when you have proved that your business works and is established with regular orders and a positive cashflow. In situations like this it is very easy to convince yourself that you need to make purchases that really you don't. Be honest with yourself, and if possible, run your provisional shopping list past an experienced adviser. He or she will be able to take an objective view and dissuade you from buying or leasing things you do not really need.

At the same time, do not make the mistake of scrimping on items that really are crucial. There is little point in making do with a computer that keeps on crashing or has insufficient power or memory to work effectively. Similarly, if you need particular tools to take your products to a saleable standard, it makes sense to budget for this at start-up.

It is worth taking time when you are researching and buying start-up equipment. Always shop around for the best deals,

and do not be afraid to negotiate with sellers. The worst thing they can do is say 'no', and if you are buying a number of items from a particular retailer (say, a computer, a printer, and some office furniture) you ought to ask for a discount as a matter of course. Again, do not be afraid to negotiate this, and do not feel cheeky asking for some freebies: if you have just spent £2,000 at your local computer outlet, the staff are not (within reason) going to mind throwing in some free software, discs or printer paper.

" In most business sectors there is a healthy market in reconditioned equipment. "

With the possible exception of IT equipment, for which prices are so competitive anyway, you should also consider whether you really need new equipment or whether you could get by just as effectively with second-hand items, which should save you a substantial amount of cash. In most business sectors there is a healthy market in reconditioned equipment. Keep an eye on your profession's trade press, or have a surf around internet sites like eBay. However, if you do this, think carefully about buying 'sight unseen' from a remote trade vendor or over the internet. Make sure you have sufficient guarantees of the quality of the items you are buying. Established eBay sellers are rated for their quality of goods and service, but if you are buying through an advertisement in a magazine where there are fewer guarantees, you will need to be careful that you are getting good-quality equipment. It is better to spend a day driving to check out a piece of equipment with your own eyes than to buy sight unseen and regret it afterwards.

It is also important to consider the image of your equipment in a public-facing business. Customers' perceptions will have a major effect on referrals and repeat business. A van does not need to be brand new to be perfectly acceptable among your customers. However, a rusty old banger is not going to give your customers as much confidence as a clean white van with your logo and details professionally painted on the side.

It can work the other way around, too. If you arrive at meetings in a flash car with a personalised plate, your potential customer may think that you are making more profit than you should, and that they might get a better deal elsewhere. You will find that customer perceptions and your brand (see Chapter 7) can be the first things to take a knock if you make false economies. Do not be afraid of investing in a profile that is likely to improve your business. Just take some time and put some thought into making sure it is the right profile.

Research pays

When you are thinking about your start-up capital, you should always consider the return on investment a particular purchase offers you. It can be very expensive to buy

Jargon Buster

Public-facing A business that works with the public on a daily basis. Includes shops, service and repair businesses and several other categories.

the wrong thing, so do some research to make sure you do not. When you are purchasing non-specialist equipment, take into account the many online review sites that exist, and consult publications such as the *Which?* consumer magazines to ensure that when you start shopping you are buying the right items at the right price.

❝ Give suppliers the option of matching or beating their competitors. ❞

Draw up a list of criteria against which you can judge the value of each purchase. You should include factors such as price, availability, location, delivery time, credit terms, training, after-sales support and guarantees. If the suppliers you would like to do business with are some of the more expensive in the marketplace, do some research on prices and give them the option of matching or beating their competitors. No-one wants to lose business, particularly on high capital items, or from a customer who may be coming back for more. Always ask for a better deal.

It is also worthwhile saving one aspect of negotiation to the end when everything else is agreed. A staged repayment schedule can help your cashflow and often will not make much difference to sellers, they are still getting the business out of you, after all. Ask if you can split payment into thirds. For example, you put a third down, pay a third in 30 days' time and the balance by the end of the next month. Sellers that are keen to do business should be open to negotiation.

WORKING CAPITAL

Working capital is the money you need to run your business. If you manufacture your products this will include the purchase of raw materials and the cost of converting them into saleable products. It also includes day-to-day and recurring costs, such as:

- Utility, phone and internet bills.
- Insurance.
- Stationery and postage.
- Travel, hospitality and accommodation costs.
- The money you need to survive until you can start to draw cash.

Make sure you have enough money to finance your business until it is established, this could take one month or it could take twelve. If you have planned your business carefully (see Chapter 5), you should have a reasonable idea of when this will be, but it pays to be a little on the pessimistic side and, if possible, reserve more working capital than your plans suggest. This will give you a bit of breathing space if something goes wrong or business does not take off as fast as you had hoped.

Do not forget to take into account the time it takes you to actually get paid. In an ideal world every client would pay out five minutes after receiving an invoice; sadly things do not often work out like that. Because of the inevitable lag between delivery and payment (unless you are dealing direct with consumers in cash, of course), even when your business is up and running, you may find that you have orders but struggle to finance them. This is frequently referred to as 'over-trading'. When you are putting together your business plan you need to think about this carefully. Over-trading can be a particular problem for new businesses. You may be swamped with orders from day one, but until the cash starts flowing it can be tough to finance or manage it effectively.

Do not forget that you need to pay yourself. When you are working for yourself in a small operation, whether you are a sole trader or limited company, your personal finances are very closely linked to your business finances. If your business is not bringing in the cash in the first few months and you have not put some money aside or established credit facilities, you are not just going to struggle to pay your day-to-day running costs, you will also struggle to feed yourself and pay the mortgage.

 The subject of working capital is closely tied up with cashflow management, in the day-to-day running of your business. For more information on cashflow, see Chapter 10.

Keeping down costs

As with start-up capital, keeping down the amount you spend means cutting out non-essentials, and doing some research and negotiation. Remember that you should apply these principles to your personal living costs too.

When it comes to acquiring services that are billed on a recurring basis (insurance, utilities, phone and internet and even your mortgage and personal loans), it can really pay to either shop around or to approach a broker. Particularly in the sphere of insurance or finance, a broker can help you find the very best deals, possibly combining your personal and business insurance plans to achieve a discount. Many brokers operate on a no-fee basis (they take a commission on services sold), and a good one should be able to save you significant amounts of money. It is easy to save a few pounds every month on recurring expenses, and this can add up to several hundred pounds a year. When you are in the early stages of working for yourself, a few extra pounds can make all the difference, so it is worth shopping around for the best possible deals before you start.

When you are dealing with suppliers, always negotiate. Business-to-business suppliers expect you to negotiate, and might form a negative opinion of your business abilities if you do not. Make reasonable offers, always bearing in mind that the supplier needs to make money but will be hoping to win long-term business from you. When appropriate, discuss quantity discounts, and if the circumstances are right, ask your suppliers

> ❝ Saving a few pounds every month on recurring expenses and this can add up to several hundred pounds a year. ❞

how they can help with marketing materials, back-up and customer support. Major product suppliers will have dedicated trade support and many will have a wide range of marketing materials, from brochures to shop displays.

Discuss the possibility of buying on a sale-or-return basis. If a supplier accepts a sale-or-return deal, it will sometimes be on the understanding that you are compensated for any products you return with a credit note rather than cash. Even if this is the case, such an arrangement gives your business flexibility and allows you to experiment with product ranges to find out what works best for your target market.

When you have negotiated a deal that suits you, make sure that you confirm all orders in writing clearly stating the product details, price, credit terms, delivery method and time. If time of delivery is critical to your schedule, insert a 'time of essence' statement into your order. This allows you to cancel the contract should your suppliers fail to deliver the product on time.

Raising the money

There are many different sources for finance so make sure you take into account all your options. You'll only need to secure start-up finance once, so it is worth researching any opportunities to save cash or take advantage of grants.

The three basic types of start-up finance are:

- **Equity finance.** The money you put into the business yourself, or persuade an investor or business partner to contribute in exchange for a share of the profits.

- **Grants.** These are available from a variety of public bodies and other organisations.

- **Debt finance.** Bank loans and cash from overdrafts and credit cards.

Grants

There are thousands of grants available to businesses in the UK. They are usually designed for specific types of business, or targeted at entrepreneurs in special interest groups (the young, the unemployed, ex-offenders), particular market sectors or particular areas of the country.

Grants are most commonly available for investment purposes, and to help secure essential equipment or assets. Because there is such a wide variety of grants on offer, you may well be eligible for one. They include grants and awards such as New Entrepreneur Scholarships, Crafts Council Development Awards and Film Tax Relief. Your local Business Link will help you find the right grant and take you through the application process, which can often be very involved. To get an initial idea of what's available you can search the Grants and Support Directory (GSD), which can be found in the Finance and Grants section of the Business Link website.

Dent finance

If you choose debt finance, then regardless of the size of loan, there are benefits in shopping around. Banks often offer competitive charges and (in most cases) a period of free banking when you first open your account. The obvious place to start looking for finance is the bank where you have your personal current account, or your business account if you have already opened one. However, even if you have a good relationship with your current bank there are benefits to looking at other banks too:

For further information on business grants see www.businesslink.org.uk

- It offers the opportunity to practise presenting your business. You might also get some useful feedback and criticism from a bank manager who has never had any dealings with you before.
- Forming relationships with a number of lenders in the early days can come in useful later on. At a local level, finding a bank manager who is enthusiastic about your business and your potential is extremely beneficial. Spreading your financial 'shopping' between banks makes it easier to discover these individuals.
- It is not necessarily a good idea to have all your accounts and financing with a single bank. For example, if you struggle to meet repayments on a loan, your bank could place restrictions on the other services it offers you. Equally, you will find it much harder to extend the loan on your personal account if your bank manager knows your business is in trouble. Spreading your financial services needs among banks keeps you in control to a much greater degree.
- When your business is established, having a relationship with more than one bank or funder also gives you more scope. Just as you negotiate with other suppliers, you can negotiate with your bank when it comes to interest rates and pricing. Banking is a competitive

> ❝ Forming relationships with a number of lenders in the early days can come in useful later on. ❞

Case Study Janice

Janice is a Personal Assistant to the Managing Director of an engineering company. She is married with one child, and currently earns £18,000 p.a. Unfortunately, the crèche in her village is closing, and because she places a high value on good care for her son she has decided to work from home as a self-employed virtual PA.

Janice already has three contacts who have agreed to use her services on a retainer, and is confident she can win more. To offer a truly effective service she needs a spacious, high-specification office. She decides to spend £4,000 converting her garage for the purpose.

She goes to the bank and explains she is investing £2,000 of her own money. The bank manager is impressed by her detailed business plan and P&L and cashflow forecasts. He agrees to a personal loan of £2,500, which also clears her outstanding credit card debt.

sector, and you might find your bank manager is willing to equal (or better) offers from rival banks.

OVERDRAFTS

If you expect to be able to pay borrowed funds back reasonably quickly, an overdraft on your business account is an ideal solution. It can be a good idea to have overdrafts on both your business and personal accounts, allowing you to finance and keep track of living expenses

Pros and cons of overdrafts

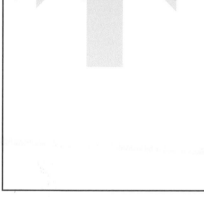

Pros

You only pay for what you use. If your overdraft limit is £1,000 but your account is permanently in credit it will not cost you anything.

Overdrafts are flexible. Providing you stay within your agreed limit, you can dip in and out of credit as and when you wish. For example, if you want to settle a bill for £1,000 but you only have £800 in the bank, you can draw the extra £200 you need from your overdraft facility.

Cons

Exceeding your overdraft limit, can be expensive. In addition to paying extra interest rates, sometimes as high as 29.5 per cent, the bank may also bounce your cheques and your direct debits. This can damage your reputation, cost you money and waste your time getting it sorted.

Exceeding your overdraft limit may also result in steep administration charges. At the time of writing, many bank customers are challenging these charges on legal grounds, and it may soon be the case that banks cease to charge large administration fees on unauthorised overdrafts. However, banks are commercial organisations, and if this does happen, the chances are they will look for another way to discourage unauthorised borrowing.

Your bank can withdraw your overdraft at any time, and it is most likely to do this when you are least able to cope with it.

and business expenses separately. In fact, even if you do not initially need an overdraft, there are benefits in negotiating one anyway. It's much easier to put one in place when you are in a strong financial position. Use your cashflow

forecasts supported by a strong profit & loss account to show that an overdraft facility would make sense.

While overdrafts are generally easy to arrange, the downside is that the bank can also withdraw them at anytime. It is

The FSA is the independent body that regulates the financial services industry in the UK. To help you shop around for financial products or to check that the firm you want to deal with is authorised by the FSA see www.fsa.gov.uk

unlikely to do this when your business is doing well, but again, if things go wrong withdrawal becomes a possibility. This is another good reason for keeping your personal and business accounts with different banks.

Remember that if you are a sole trader, overdrafts (like all forms of finance) are your personal liability. If you are a new limited company, and you require a significant loan and an overdraft, it's likely the bank will require security. In both instances, if you are unable to repay the debt, the bank can take you to court and seize your assets.

BUSINESS LOANS

One alternative to an overdraft is a loan, agreed for a set period with a defined monthly payment. With larger loans, the bank is likely to ask for security, which generally means a second charge on your house. This is a step that you need to think about seriously, and it is worthwhile seeking legal advice. Be wary about taking a secured business loan from the same bank that provides your mortgage. It puts you entirely in the hands of one institution, without the benefit of a single low rate of interest. On the other hand, re-mortgaging to release equity can be a very cost-effective way of raising money, but only

if you can pay back the capital over a shorter period than your mortgage term. One important factor here is timing. Getting a mortgage without a guaranteed income can be difficult, so if you are planning to use the equity in your house it is wise to plan well ahead and get the money in the bank before you need it.

Interest

The interest rate will vary dependent on the size of the loan. For larger loans, it is sometimes possible to arrange to pay interest only for an initial period and then, after an agreed period, start making capital repayments. If the loan is secured you should benefit from a better interest rate. Remember to find out what fees there are, if any, and to check early repayment penalties.

One benefit of a loan is that it allows you to finance major purchases separately from your overdraft, which can be kept free for day-to-day running and emergencies. It is always vitally important to have a bit of slack in the system. Making a habit of spending right up to your overdraft limit every month reduces the amount of slack, leaving you vulnerable when things go wrong. Many self-employed people choose a loan to finance their start-up while using an overdraft to increase their available working capital. Doing this allows you to exploit the respective strengths of each form of finance.

When you are shopping around for loans, do not forget to check the internet. In recent years many banks (especially the former building societies) have offered online loans at substantially lower rates

"Re-mortgaging to release equity can be a very cost-effective way of raising money. "

Pros and cons of loans

Pros	Cons
Unlike an overdraft, you have to make regular payments to reduce the amount owed. This may not sound like an advantage, but it prevents you from 'drifting' on repayments and letting your debt mount to a point where it is unmanageable.	The bank will expect you to show that you are making a similar, if not larger, financial commitment than you are asking them to. This may be in the form of cash, equipment, or stock, and needs to demonstrate that you are prepared to back your own judgement.
Providing you meet the repayments, a loan cannot be withdrawn.	You must make repayments on the full amount, regardless of what you use. This could be expensive if the money is just sitting in your account. The cheapest loan will still have a higher interest rate than the best bank account.
You do not have to give the lender a stake in your business or a share of your profits.	
Interest rates may be fixed for the term so you will know the level of repayments throughout the life of the loan.	Some loans have early redemption fees to be paid if you settle ahead of schedule.
You may be able to negotiate lower, interest-only payments at the start of the repayment plan. After a set period you will then make capital and interest repayments.	In many cases, banks will want to secure larger loans against your assets, which generally means your home. If you fail to make the payments, the bank could force you to sell your property.

than are available in branches. In general, these preferential rates have mainly been available for personal rather than business loans. However, if you only need a relatively small amount, say just a few thousand pounds, it may make sense to research cheap personal loans from online providers. There are a number of websites that allow you to compare the best rates on loans, including The Motley Fool (www.fool.co.uk) and Quick Compare (www.quickcompare.co.uk). You can also find comparison charts of different lenders' rates in the personal finance sections of many sunday newspapers. Bear in mind that most comparison services compare personal rather than business loans. However, if you only need to borrow a few thousand pounds and you have a good credit score, a personal loan may be the quickest and the most convenient route.

Guarantees and liabilities

For larger loans, banks and major creditors will usually require personal guarantees, formalised in a contract, on any loan they make. If you are a sole trader, this means the full responsibility will fall on you. In a larger operation the risk may be spread between the other directors or partners and major shareholders, and often both.

Limited liability status generally protects shareholders in the business from being sued by the business's creditors. However, when a personal guarantee for a bank loan is issued, the individual shareholder (which if you are the sole shareholder means you) can be held personally liable for the debt.

Case Study   Keith

Keith has worked as a domestic appliance service engineer for 15 years. He is employed by a large business that holds service contracts with several major domestic appliance retailers. Keith's job is secure, but he is not entirely happy. He has a large area to cover and no control over his work diary, so he spends hours on the road driving from one end of his patch to another.

He is pretty sure he can manage his time better than his employers do, so he decides to set up his own service business. He has plenty of regular customers whom he is sure would be much more happier paying him direct than they are paying his employer, not least because he is planning to charge lower prices.

To give him a head start, Keith has the opportunity to acquire the existing domestic appliance business of his friend Bob, who is retiring. Bob's business, which is valued at £35,000, includes a van, tools, brand identity and, most valuable of all, a long list of customers that Keith can add to his existing customer base.

Keith looks at his finances as they stand:

- His house is valued at £185,000 with £20,000 outstanding on the mortgage.
- He owes his credit card companies £7,500.
- Keith's wife, Sara, has £3,200 of outstanding debt on store cards.
- He has £3,500 remaining to pay off on a bank loan he used to buy a new car a year previously.

Keith decides that the most practical solution is to free up some of the £165,000 equity in his house by taking out a mortgage while he is still working. He plans to become self-employed in 12 months' time, when Bob finally retires.

His current outstanding debt is £34,200. Total repayments are £557 per month. He takes out a £65,000 mortgage on his house, with a monthly repayment of £575. This allows him to:

- Clear his existing debts.
- Buy Bob's business.
- Put £5,000 in the bank to cover any extra start-up costs and to use as initial working capital.

The refinance allows him to start his business and put himself on a sounder financial footing personally, all for an extra £18 per month.

You should always take care when giving personal guarantees, and wherever possible, try to ensure that they only apply to specific debts or loans. A widely drawn guarantee could mean you are liable for all of the losses of the business. However, the Banking Code states that borrowing must not be for an unlimited amount. Carefully check the terms of any contract you sign, and especially if the loan is for a large amount, consider seeking professional advice. If the loan is from a major lender it is unlikely there will be anything seriously amiss, but a good solicitor will explain all the implications of the agreement you are signing in a wholly neutral way.

In some situations, particularly if you are new in business or you have a poor credit rating, a bank is likely to ask for a guarantor. This is a responsible individual against whom the bank will claim should you default on your loan payments.

Virtually anyone can act as a guarantor for a loan, providing they can prove to the bank that they have the financial resources to back up their guarantee. Guarantors are most commonly family members, parents for example, or other individuals with whom you have a close relationship.

Rejection

If the bank turns you down, you should not necessarily count it as a vote of no confidence. Banks, in general, tend to be conservative lenders, and if your bank perceives a high level of risk in your business model it may well turn you down. However, rejections can happen for other reasons, too:

- You may not have presented your business effectively or with sufficient confidence. Your bank manager may, as a result, not have seen the true potential of your business, or possibly formed a negative opinion of your confidence and personal skills, which are vital to the success of any operation.
- You and your bank manager might not see eye-to-eye. For example, he or she may previously have had a bad experience with your type of business, which could affect his or her opinion of yours.
- You may have a poor personal credit score.

If you are rejected once, do not assume you will be rejected by every lender you approach.

❝ If you are rejected once, do not assume you will be rejected by every lender you approach. ❞

To find a solicitor in your area, contact the Law Society. See www.lawsociety.org.uk or useful addresses page 205 for further details.

Take a look at your presentation, your plan and your basic model, and perhaps talk to a business adviser about how they can be improved.

If you believe in your business and know there is a profitable market, you must keep trying. Many of today's successful businesses were rejected when they first went for finance.

Career Development Loans

If you need to fund vocational training to enhance your skills or qualifications prior to launching your business, you may be able to benefit from a Career Development Loan (CDL). A CDL is partly financed by the Learning and Skills Council (LSC) through an arrangement with Barclays, The Co-operative Bank and The Royal Bank of Scotland.

You can take out a CDL regardless of whether you are employed, self-employed or unemployed, and borrow from £300 to £8,000 to help you fund up to two years of learning (or up to three years if

❝If you need to fund vocational training to enhance your skills or qualifications prior to launching your business, you may be able to benefit from a Career Development Loan. ❞

the course includes one year of relevant practical work experience). The LSC will pay the interest on your loan while you are learning, after which you repay the loan over an agreed period. Your CDL can help cover your course fees, course costs such as books, equipment, and travel expenses and living expenses.

CREDIT CARDS

Having a credit card or two can be a very useful way of paying for short term purchases. If you have had a personal bank account for a while there is a good chance you will already have a credit card, or have been offered one by your bank. There are several good deals on credit cards online, or you may also be able to get one tied to your business account. A personal credit card is a good way of paying your living expenses for the first few months of self-employment, so you do not have to worry about taking cash out of your business. In general, credit card companies will only increase your limit if you prove to be a good customer by regularly sending cash their way and sticking around long enough to be hit by interest payments. Show fickleness in your allegiance and they will be less co-operative.

A good compromise that will see your credit limit climb steadily is to stick around for a year or more, paying off your debt regularly. Most of the time you will be interest-free, but if you give the lender

For advice on Career Development Loans, call the CDL Information Line on 0800 585 505 or see the Education and Learning section on www.direct.gov.uk or the Learning and Skills Council website, www.lsc.gov.uk

Pros and cons of credit cards

Pros

You only pay interest on the amount you borrow.

If you pay your full balance off every month, it costs you nothing and helps your cashflow.

If a card company suspects that you are using its card in this way it cannot actually stop you. It is as bound by the terms of the agreement as you are, but it might be much less helpful when you approach them about extensions to your credit limit.

Because the market is so competitive, many cards have interest-free introductory periods on both usage and on balances transferred from other cards and accounts. You could use a card to pay your living expenses for the 0% offer period and then transfer the balance to another card as your business begins to make money. However, credit card companies are beginning to get wise to this sort of strategy, and it may not be a practical option forever. A separate card makes it easier to keep business and personal expenses apart.

If you make your repayments on time, it helps to establish a good credit record.

It is relatively easy to transfer balances from one card to another (although there is usually a charge of 1-3 per cent of the transferred balance for doing so).

Cons

Rates of interest on credit cards tend to be crippling. If you run into trouble and cannot pay off or transfer the balance, you can wind up paying some hefty fees.

It is easy to spend on credit cards. You should try to be cautious with a credit card and always spend borrowed money as if it is your own.

You need a relatively good credit score to get a credit card with a reasonable credit limit.

To a find business angel, contact the British Business Angels Association. See www.bbaa.org.uk or useful addresses page 200 for further details.

a trickle of profit it is more likely to see you as a good bet for the future, and extend your limit. Another strategy is to simply ring them up and announce that you are thinking of transferring your balance to a 0% scheme on a different card, but that you might change your mind if your credit limit is increased. If you have been a good customer, they will probably go along with you. Remember that 'buying' credit is just like buying anything else from any other supplier, everything is negotiable.

INCUBATORS

A business incubator is an organisation devoted to nurturing and developing small businesses. Typically, incubators may offer office or workspace, management support, training and assistance with financing. Although incubators can be run as private businesses, many are quasi-public organisations.

Many incubators specialise in particular sectors, such as technology or design. They are often, but not always, associated with universities, having been set up to assist enterprising and innovative graduates and postgraduates as a development of a research product (a situation sometimes referred to as a 'spin-out' rather than a 'start-up'). Incubators are also operated by trusts and organisations.

BUSINESS ANGELS

These are typically experienced business people who have spare capital to invest, and usually, a certain amount of spare time that they are also prepared to invest in mentoring new businesses. Angels are most likely to be interested in businesses that have a strong potential for growth, so if your idea of self-employment involves staying small and not taking on staff, it is unlikely that you will find an angel that is interested in your operation. Business angels tend to work on the basis that they are lending money to an enterprise in which they will have a say in running. If an angel thinks you are just going to take his or her money and refuse any advice, they are unlikely to help you.

If you do have a business model based on strong growth, you will probably find

---

Incubators in the UK

This is a small, random selection of the many different incubators found in the UK:

www.ukbi.co.uk – UK incubator resources.

www.carbontrust.co.uk/technology/incubator – a business incubator operated by The Carbon Trust, a government-owned company that works with business to reduce carbon emissions.

www.bangor.ac.uk/innovation/enterprise/ – business incubation and enterprise unit at the University of Wales, Bangor.

www.brainspark.com – an incubator specialising in information technology businesses.

www.stjohns.co.uk – incubator unit offering office space and business mentoring in Cambridge.

❝ If you do have a business model based on strong growth, you will probably find that a business angel is a lot better, more experienced and more helpful than the average high street bank manager. ❞

that a business angel is a lot better, more experienced and more helpful than the average high street bank manager. Angel investments tend to vary between £10,000 and £750,000. Where larger amounts are required, this can be organised though a syndicate of personal contacts or a business angel network. The lead investor in a syndicate (sometimes referred to as the archangel) would generally be the one that actually gets involved in the business. But the archangel could also call on other investors for additional expertise where required.

Business angels can be involved at most stages of business development, but because they want to capitalise on their investments they are more likely to be interested in business that is in its early stages or beginning a period of

expansion. Because of the level of personal involvement, most business angels prefer to invest in companies within a reasonable distance of their homes, but for specialist or technology companies that may not apply.

Unlike banks, angels can take a more entrepreneurial approach to investment. They will look at you, your market and the opportunity. They would take the following points into consideration:

- Do you have the necessary expertise and track record to succeed?
- What is the competitive edge or unique selling point of your business?
- What is the growth potential and characteristics of the market?
- Are their skills and experience compatible with you and your team?
- How committed are you? What financial commitment are you making?
- What is the exit plan? In other words, at what point will they get a return on their investment?

When you are looking for an angel, it is important that you consider compatibility. It is great to have the money, but as business angels are generally rather 'hands on' in their approach it is important that their skills and expertise match your own, in addition to you both sharing the same objectives for the business.

Jargon Buster

Business angel A private investor who brings both expertise and equity finance to start-ups.

103

FRIENDS AND FAMILY

It is also worth considering family and friends as a source for raising finance. This type of funding can provide a fast, affordable solution to your loan requirements.

However, do not expect friends or family to fall over themselves in their bid to get involved in your business venture. They can vary in their commitment from being your biggest supporters to being a touch envious of your venture, or even positively against you taking such a risk.

When presenting your case to your friends or family, it is important to present the opportunity properly and make them aware of the risks as well as the potential. If you have already been turned down by the bank, outline the reasons why, and emphasise to your potential lender that they should not lend you any more than they can afford to lose.

It is also worthwhile drawing up a simple agreement, which should include any details of loan repayments. This helps formalise the arrangement and prevent the misunderstandings that can arise from verbal agreements.

Jargon Buster

Credit reference agency An agency such as Experian, Equifax and Callcredit, which shares information with banks and lending agencies on an individual's credit history. Individuals have a legal right to access the data that is held on them.

Managing loan finance

Loans require a great deal of responsibility. You cannot just get one and then forget about it. In this section we are going to consider how you can protect your loan and stay on the right side of your lender in case you need extra funding.

YOUR CREDIT SCORE

We have already mentioned the concept of your credit score, so it is worth taking a detailed look at what it actually means. By mutual agreement, lenders share information between themselves about the credit worthiness of individuals and companies. The data is compiled by credit reference agencies and made available to all corporate lenders.

A credit score is not an assessment of how potentially profitable you are for a lender in terms of your inclinations to run up debt and pay it off at high rates of interest. It is hardly in the interest of lenders to share that kind of information with their competitors. Your credit score is the lending industry's collective perception of the risk you represent, that is, how likely you are to default on a loan. If you have a good credit score you should have no problem raising finance.

However, if you set-up a limited company, you are effectively starting from scratch as far as a credit score is concerned. This is because your personal financial situation is legally separate from that of your company, which is technically regarded in its own right, with its own credit record. In these circumstances, even if you do not need finance, it is worth considering taking out a small business loan to establish a credit record. Similarly it is worth taking a company charge card and paying the balance at the end of every month.

When you become self-employed, you can expect your personal credit rating to take a temporary dip. The reasons for this are easy to understand. If you have left a full-time job to start your own business, you have no longer got a guaranteed income. This is a critical part of the lending industry's scoring criteria, as with no regular income, you are more likely to experience financial problems or default on loans. You are, consequently, a greater risk as far as lenders are concerned.

❝ If you have a good credit score, you should have no problem in raising finance. ❞

LOAN INSURANCE

It is increasingly common for loan providers to recommend that you take out loan repayment insurance to cover repayments in the event that you are unable to work owing to ill health. This

You do not necessarily have to insure a financial product with the lender you have secured it from, (though naturally the lender will encourage you to do just that). In some cases, you may be able to save as much as 75 per cent of the premium by using a specialist protection plan.

adds to the cost of the loan but it is worth considering. If you are using a financial broker, he or she will be able to advise you on the best insurance deal.

Remember sick pay as such doesn't exist in self-employment, so if you fall off a ladder and break your leg, how will you pay the mortgage and the credit card bills? Cost effective cover for accident or sickness is well worth considering. Talk to your broker or visit insurance deals websites such as www.paymentcare.co.uk or www.moneysupermarket.com.

The Small Firms' Loan Guarantee

If you are planning to become self-employed and you have a sound business plan and an interested lender, but you do not have the assets for a secured loan, it is worth considering The Small Firms' Loan Guarantee scheme.

The scheme is supported by all the major banks, who between them administer the eligibility criteria and make the commercial decisions. If you are accepted on to the scheme the Government effectively secures 75 per cent of your loan in exchange for a 2 per cent premium on the outstanding balance of the loan, payable to the Department for Business, Enterprise and Regulatory Reform (DBERR).

There are some restrictions, but in general the scheme is available for most business types and most purposes for businesses up to five years old. The loans can be up to a maximum of £250,000 with terms of up to ten years.

❝ In general the Small Firms' Loan Guarantee is available for most business types and most purposes for businesses that are up to five years old. ❞

 To find an insurance broker in your area, contact the British Insurance Brokers Association. See www.biba.org.uk or useful addresses page 201 for further details.

Advertising and marketing

Selling your products and services is what business is all about. To do it effectively you need to understand your market and appreciate how its individual members view your product. Above all, you need to discover the best ways to promote your business and communicate with your customers. This chapter will help you understand the jargon and get under the skin of advertising and marketing.

Why are advertising and marketing important?

Businesses often neglect advertising and marketing, but they do so at their peril. Not devoting enough time and resources to effective promotion is one of the major reasons for business failure.

You are not going to last very long in self-employment if nobody knows you are running a business. It is very easy to get so caught up in creating and providing your product or service that you forget to maintain your profile or search for new customers. Plenty of conscientious self-employed people will tell you that they spend so much time looking after a small number of existing customers that they fail to invest time looking for new ones.

This is a risky way of doing business. Building new relationships is not simply a method of expanding your business, it is also insurance against the day when your current clients disappear. The more widely-known and respected you are, the more likely it is that you will be able to survive the times when business is slack or when you lose a major customer.

66 Building lasting relationships is key. The more widely-known and respected you are, the more likely you will be able to survive slack times. 99

Saying that, the process of marketing your business is not just a case of telling as many people as possible. Unless you are selling products to a mass market, as a small business you are much more likely to achieve success by targeting a tightly defined or local market. In that kind of situation, spreading the word as widely as possible is inefficient. The trick is to spread it as precisely as possible. To do that you need to define your market as exactly as you can and discover the most effective ways of communicating with it.

Before we go any further, we need to establish the meaning of a few terms. The whole practice of marketing is littered with jargon. It is useful to have an understanding of these terms, not least because they can often be used in a misleading way.

The most important thing to understand is that advertising and marketing are not the same thing. Advertising is just the most visible (and, often, the most expensive) part of marketing.

Jargon Buster | Common marketing terms defined

Target market The group of consumers or businesses who have a need or a desire for your product, as well as the means and willingness to pay for it. A business may have just one target market or several.

Niche marketing Refining your product offer and marketing approach so they appeal to a very narrow, specific group of potential customers, a 'niche'. Tie Rack is a niche retailer, before it existed you could only buy ties in menswear shops or department stores. Aiming at a niche means you can specialise and create an offer more likely to appeal to your customers. Saga started as a niche travel company. Starbucks went for a niche market in refreshments; coffee shops. That niche is now a major sector in its own right.

Advertising The part of marketing that deals with directly persuading members of your target market to buy your product or service.

Brand The reputation and character of your business and product, or both, in the eyes of your target market.

Brand values The qualities you want your target market to associate with your brand. Brand values may include value, reliability, friendliness, speed of service and many other characteristics. Most businesses concentrate on developing three or four key brand values.

Marketing The process of learning about your target market and communicating with it. Marketing can also be said to include some elements of product development and presentation.

Marketing materials The print or digital materials you produce to support your marketing effort. They include your website, but the term is more usually used to describe printed items like brochures and flyers. They are also sometimes referred to as 'marketing collateral'.

Offer A potentially confusing term because it means different things to marketers and consumers. If you are shopping in Tesco and you notice that baked beans are 'on offer', you know it means that their price has been discounted. However, in marketing it is simply the word used to refer to a combination of the product and its price that you are presenting to your target market. (See "The Four Ps", on page 114.)

POS An acronym standing for Point of Sale. This is where customers are presented with marketing materials at the point where they buy your product. This may be a flyer positioned next to the till in a shop, or a marketing freebie given to the customer along with the product or service they purchase.

You and your market

Before you can sell anything, or even develop your product or service properly, you need to pin down who you are selling it to. In this section we are going to look at how you identify your target customers and sell to them.

MARKET RESEARCH

Market research is one of the most valuable (and too often underused) tools available to small businesses. Many agencies specialise in offering market research services to businesses. However you do not need to employ an agency to do it or spend a fortune. If you are running a small business you can usually research your market quite quickly and cheaply. Good research not only helps you to identify whether or not a market exists for your proposed product and service. It forces you to get to know that market, to understand its needs and desires, and begin to get a sense of how to approach it.

To research a market thoroughly you need to:

- Determine whether a market exists for your proposed product or service.
- Identify ways to tailor your product or service to fit the needs of the market.
- Find out the best ways of advertising and selling to the market.
- Investigate any additional opportunities that crop up as a result of your research.

Getting started

Few businesses start by being the first to find 'a gap in the market', so one of the best ways to identify opportunities is to look at what other businesses are doing. If there are others doing what you plan to do, then the chances are there is definitely a market out there for your services. The secret is to look and learn from your competitors, although copying is not the answer. If you blindly go and offer exactly the same product or service as your competitors, in exactly the same way, you may struggle to establish yourself.

It is important to let the market dictate the nature of your offer rather than creating it and expecting people to come flocking. Too many businesses start off by creating a product or service and only then start thinking about the best way to find a market for it. A far better approach is to identify the market and work out its needs first. You can then create your offer in light of what you have learned.

Depending on your business and your experience, you may already have enough knowledge of your market to warrant just a small amount of research. For example, if you are setting up as an independent consultant in an industry you have worked

Case Study | Annette

Annette is a skilled horticulturist and garden designer. She wants to set up a garden design business, but is not quite sure what services to offer and how best to promote herself. She decides to do some market research to try to find out what the market is like for garden services within a ten-mile radius of her home.

She starts by identifying a couple of areas that have houses with large gardens and a generally affluent population. Initially she considers posting a questionnaire to a few dozen randomly selected addresses in the areas she has identified. However, she is concerned about the depth of the possible response, as she is most interested in detailed feedback on her idea. So, using her network of friends, she negotiates introductions to half a dozen families living in her target areas. She pops round to ask them a few questions at a pre-arranged time, thanking each set of interviewees with a bottle of wine for their time and contribution.

The people she interviews can, of course, not only answer questions on their own behalf, but give her useful information about what other people in the locality are saying about their gardens. From her questioning and other research, three interesting facts emerge:

- Following the popularity of home and garden makeover shows on TV, many local residents have an interest in designed and landscaped gardens.
- Many residents complain they do not have enough time to look after their gardens.
- There are already professional gardeners in the area who are kept very busy. However, most of them simply mow lawns and do other time-consuming, but basic, garden chores. None offers a garden design service, though many will do landscaping work to someone else's plans.

Annette concludes there is a market for her garden design skills both with garden owners and with other professional gardeners who may wish to include her landscaping and design service as an add-on to their existing businesses. Thinking ahead, Annette also wonders if the situation is similar in other areas of the country. She could sell her design skills to homeowners nationwide, perhaps using the internet as a marketing tool.

As a result of her research efforts, Annette has developed her original idea into something appropriate to an identifiable market, and at the same time has uncovered some opportunities she had not previously considered.

in for 20 years, you probably already have a detailed knowledge of your target market. And with that knowledge, you should be able to launch a successful marketing strategy. A little further research will still be useful for you, however, such as exploring how other independent consultants present themselves to the market.

It is also worth remembering that if you are too close to a market, you may not always see the opportunities that others see from the outside. No matter how much experience you have in a particular sector, your broad understanding can benefit from investing time in market research. It is a good way of spotting new trends and niche opportunities, both of which will help you to create the most attractive targeted offers. Your best bet is to carry out some direct research, ideally by identifying members of your potential market and asking them a few questions, either face-to-face or by using a questionnaire. You may need to provide an incentive, but it does not need to be much, perhaps a special price on your product or service once you launch.

If you are conducting research among friends and colleagues, you will probably be given an opinion for free. At all times,

---

Case Study   Harpreet

Harpreet is a computer programmer. He has developed his own electronic 'shopping cart', a program that allows website visitors to use their credit cards to make purchases from ecommerce websites quickly and securely. Up until now he has been working for a small software company, but he is thinking of becoming freelance and offering his services through internet marketplace sites like Elance and Guru. Although there are many commercial and free carts in the market, Harpreet's cart offers additional benefits. He is also happy to customise existing shopping cart programs to fulfil the needs of particular customers. He has a pretty shrewd idea of what most ecommerce site owners want from a shopping cart:

- **Added value.** Harpreet knows he will be competing with cheaper providers based in Asia, so he must offer his UK customers an added value service that differentiates him from his competitors.
- **Ease of use.** Owners of ecommerce websites are keenly aware of the fact that a badly-

designed or confusing interface can result in lost sales.

- **Security.** Users of ecommerce sites, webmasters and the banks that provide the merchant accounts, prefer electronic shopping carts that are secure and reliable.

Harpreet does not assume that he knows everything about his target market. This is a healthy attitude for anyone considering self-employment. So he goes online and posts questions in forums such as www.sitepoint.net, which he knows are heavily used by owners of ecommerce businesses.

He learns useful lessons from the responses. As well as value, ease of use and security, Harpreet discovers that time is a critical factor for webmasters under pressure from clients to exploit new online trends. A high value is placed on responsiveness and turnaround times. Harpreet adjusts his provisional business plan to take account of these factors, packaging an offer than combines technical expertise with fast delivery and an emphasis on high-level customer service.

however, ask for critical feedback, particularly from people you know well. You do not want anyone telling you just what they think you want to hear.

When you are approaching members of a possible target market, take care to frame the questions you ask in the right way. Questions than can be answered with a simple 'yes' or 'no' are not as much use to you as their wider opinion. Rather than asking whether someone is happy with an existing supplier, ask what the most frustrating thing about that supplier's service is, how it could be improved and what aspects of it they are most happy with.

THE RIGHT PRODUCT

Based on your skills and initial understanding of the market, it is likely that you already have a fairly good idea of what kind of product or service you are going to offer, before you start your market research. So it is often more useful to think of market research as being the second stage of a three stage product development process. It might seem a bit silly talking about product development if you are launching a one-man business, but it does not need to be complicated or time consuming:

Stage 1: Define your product or service, based on your talent, experience and resources.
Stage 2: Research potential markets to find out what the demand is like for the type of product or service you're proposing to offer, and to identify additional needs or weaknesses you may not have previously thought of.

Stage 3: Refine your product or service in the light of what you have found out during your market research.

Stages two and three of the define-research-refine process can, and should, be repeated throughout the life of your business. You should always be on the lookout for ways to improve your product or service in response to demand. Creating an offer that appeals to your target market is critical to your success.

Segmentation

It is also important to remember that not everyone in your group of target customers will have exactly the same needs. In fact, it may be possible to divide your customers into sections according to their specific needs. In marketing terms, these are known as segments. Segmentation is the process of making slight changes in your product or your marketing approach depending on which segment of your market you are targeting. Segmentation is a bit like dividing your wider market into a number of individual niche markets and catering for each one's needs in a slightly different way.

This is not rocket science and many small businesses cater for different market segments without even being familiar with the terminology. A bakery business that makes cakes for parties will probably not deliver the same cake to a three-year-old as it would to an octogenarian. The child and the elderly person are both in the market for cakes, but each is part of a slightly different segment that must be approached in a different way.

The four Ps

The exact nature of your product, and its price, should be dictated by the needs of the market. Do not try to tell your market what it wants, listen to what it needs. Most commonly, what your market needs will be defined as one, or more, of what is known in marketing terms as 'the four Ps': product, price, place and promotion.

- **Product.** The exact product or service you offer, based on the needs of your

---

Case Study Leo and Les

Leo and Les have a guitar shop in Leeds. As well as selling guitars, amplifiers, strings and other musical accessories, they perform repairs and maintenance. They have a reputation for being skilled and knowledgeable craftsmen who take great care to ensure that every instrument they sell is properly set-up and in the best possible condition. However, they not only have a good deal of competition in their home city, they are now facing pressure from online guitar sales.

In response they have decided to pay greater attention to their marketing and are launching a local advertising campaign geared to sell their offer more effectively to their target market. In the past, they have always considered their target market in very simple terms: guitarists and would-be guitarists in the Leeds area. However, that is a very broad and diverse group. When rethinking their marketing, they divided their market into three broad segments:

- Electric and bass guitarists who are interested in rock and pop.
- Acoustic guitarists interested in folk, country and jazz.
- Classical guitarists.

They then further segmented their market by age. They found that older players were more likely to be interested in acoustic instruments and tended to have more money to spend. Younger players were generally interested in electric instruments, and were often on a budget.

They divided their market still further by the skill of different players, beginner, intermediate and advanced, with each market having varied needs and budgets.

From thinking in very simple terms about their market ('..all the guitarists in Leeds...') Leo and Les have now realised that they are dealing with at least 18 market segments, which in turn leads them to think about marketing strategies that could specifically appeal to individuals within their broad target market. This now includes:

- Beginners' packs aimed at the 14-18 age range, consisting of a budget electric guitar and amp, a soft guitar case, and a tutorial book and DVD.
- A bi-monthly open-evening for advanced players who wish to try out high-end guitars.
- Sponsorship of a classical guitar concert.

Thinking about segmentation has helped Leo and Les redevelop their marketing strategy and revitalise their business.

114

target market. Also the variations of your product, based on the needs of different segments within that market.

- **Price.** The value you put on your product or service, based on what your research tells you your market is prepared to pay.
- **Place.** The location where your customers can buy your product. It might be a physical shop, or if you are selling online, it might be their own homes.
- **Promotion.** Your communication with your customers.

The first two Ps focus on the development of your product or service, based on market research. The second two represent your route to market.

A route to market

Finally, when you have defined your market, you need to make sure that you have a means of communicating and dealing with it. This is known as your route to market. If your potential customers all live in your local area and have a common demand, such as the need for plumbing or electrical services, your route to market is very simple. You can advertise in the local paper and *Yellow Pages* and take orders by telephone or email.

If you are selling products, or working on a larger scale, your route to market may become complex and involve third-party relationships. You might, for example, work through a high street retailer, or hire a sales agent to promote your product to customers who are normally out of your reach.

If you are selling a low-margin product or service, you need high volume sales to make a profit. But how, as a small business, are you going to promote your product to the large number of potential customers required? You may have a great product or service available at a great price, but that may not necessarily mean that sufficient customers are going to beat a path to your door. For large organisations like Sainsbury's and PC World, the route to their large target markets is a relatively simple one, they use their size to take their products to as many people as possible by opening stores in every large town.

Small, product-oriented businesses have traditionally used mail order as a route to a larger market than they have available to them in their local area. These days, the internet has revolutionised mail order sales, offering very small businesses routes to a global marketplace. However, as we will see in the next chapter, the internet can also bring its own unique challenges.

Finding your best route to market is also an integral part of advertising and promoting your business.

Winning business

The first time someone orders or buys your product or service is one of the most exciting moments of your business career. Winning business is the most rewarding part of the marketing process, but it can also be the most challenging.

If you are becoming self-employed, do not expect business to come to you. If you put advertisements in the *Yellow Pages* and then sit at home waiting for the phone to ring, it is likely that you are going to be disappointed, especially in the early stages of your business. You may get plenty of phone calls, but many will be from other businesses trying to sell you things.

Winning business means going out and looking for it. A successful marketing strategy may include advertising, but will also depend on making yourself known to potential customers and pitching offers to them without waiting for them to come to you. Before we move on to looking at the more obvious ways of winning

business that are based on advertising, we are going to take a look at a couple of techniques for finding business: direct marketing and referrals.

DIRECT MARKETING

Direct marketing or direct mail (often known as 'DM') means approaching potential customers directly, either by letter, telephone, email or, less commonly, in person.

Direct marketing is an interesting phenomenon: although many people dislike 'junk' mail, leaflets and cold calls, they can be an effective, comparatively cheap method for winning business. If you send out a thousand sales letters or leaflets and only get a one per cent response rate, that is still ten new customers for the price of a small print job and a couple of hundred pounds for delivery.

Customers who respond to a DM campaign are referred to as 'conversions', and the success of a campaign is judged by its percentage conversion rate. A good conversion rate can be considered anything above one per cent, depending on the product. A conversion rate of more than five per cent is considered exceptionally good under most circumstances. Direct

Planning point

When you are calculating the cost of acquiring a customer it's important to consider the customer's lifetime value. A customer spending £1,000 a year is potentially worth £10,000 if they stay with you for ten years. If your profit is 40 per cent this equates to £4,000 net profit. So, how much are you willing to pay to acquire them?

marketing specialists sometimes talk about 'cost per conversion' (CPC) or 'cost per acquisition', dividing the total cost of a campaign by the number of customers it wins.

One of the reasons that many businesses prefer direct marketing over traditional advertising is that the return on investment of a DM campaign can be precisely measured, down to the last penny, because it is possible to track the result of each individual mailing.

Jargon Buster

List broker An agency that retains data on tens or hundreds of thousands of individuals and businesses. A list broker will ask you about your target market and compile a list of addresses, or telephone numbers, or both, of potential customers (sometimes called 'prospects').

Before you even consider a direct marketing campaign, you need to make sure that you have really nailed down your target market. If you do not already have a list of potential contacts, you can buy one from a list broker. You are more likely to get an effective list from a broker if you can provide detailed demographic information on your target market. This is where your market research and product development comes in really handy. If

you are marketing to consumers rather than businesses you will need to consider the demographics of your target customer. Those most commonly used for direct marketing are:

- Age range.
- Size and age of family.
- Post code.
- Geographical area (city, suburbs, country).
- Household income.
- Employment status.
- Hobbies and interests.

When you are doing your market research it is useful to profile your target market. For example, if you are launching a web design business, you might find that many segments of your target market are small businesses based on suburban industrial estates. Feeding that information to a list broker can be a useful way of generating contacts that are similar to the ones you already have.

Some consumers restrict access to their contact details by signing up to the Mail Preference Service (MPS) or the Telephone Preference Service (TPS). Contacting these people for commercial purposes via mail or telephone could put you at risk of prosecution. If you are using a list broker, check to make sure they liaise with the MPS/TPS and regularly 'clean' their lists of registered individuals.

 For further information on the Mail Preference Service and the Telephone Preference Service, see www.mpsonline.org.uk

METHODS OF DIRECT MARKETING

- **Direct mail.** It might be unpopular, but it works. If it did not, it would not be a sales strategy used by so many businesses. When you launch a direct mail campaign you should take great care about the quality of your mailing list and also about the exact nature of the material you send out. Well-written sales copy is vital, and if you are not familiar with the techniques of sales writing, you should hire a professional copywriter to write it for you. It is also wise to 'split test', send out a variety of slightly different sales letters and measure which ones have the best result. This can be an effective way of learning more about what your target market responds to. We will look at the role of copywriters and testing in more detail later in the chapter. Handwritten addresses and stamped envelopes are more likely to be opened than typed and franked mail, writing them all out might be time-consuming, but you may find you get a better conversion rate.

- **Telemarketing.** Also known as 'cold calling', telemarketing uses exactly the same process as direct mail except that you telephone your prospects rather than sending them a letter. You do not need to do the hard work yourself, you can hire a telemarketing company to do it for you. The advantage of telemarketing over direct mail is that because it is a more interactive process, appointments with potential clients can be made for you and problems can be instantly addressed by a well-briefed telemarketer.

- **Direct email.** Using email to contact potential customers can be very cost-effective. Indeed, if you have your own list of email addresses, it is virtually free. However, there is a risk that commercial email might be considered to be 'spam', which is not only likely to tarnish your reputation but is also illegal. Email marketing is popular and widely-employed in the business world, but most reputable businesses only send commercial email to existing customers or prospects who have 'opted in' to mailing lists.

- **The personal approach.** Sometimes known as 'doorstepping', a direct personal approach to a household can yield results. It is a reasonable way of winning customers for small local businesses like gardeners and window cleaners, and is also used by larger companies promoting intangible products like utility transfers. For more professional businesses, doorstepping consumers is unlikely to be productive, as many consumers are wary of people selling door-to-door. However, if you are selling business-to-business, there is nothing wrong with spending time visiting businesses in the local area. How successful you are will depend on what you are selling and who your end customer is. Is it the receptionist or the managing director? If you run a sandwich company, then visiting businesses is a prime way of building a regular round. Even if you are selling professional services, personally dropping in to introduce yourself and leave brochures can be a very effective first step in building a relationship with potential customers. Once you have introduced yourself to a receptionist and built a rapport, you are more likely to get listened to when you place your first follow-up call.

REFERRALS

One of the best ways of winning new business is to have satisfied customers refer their friends and colleagues to you. Such word-of-mouth promotion (sometimes called 'relationship marketing') is priceless because your prospective customers are getting information about your business from a trusted source. Central to gaining referrals is the principle of building relationships with customers and other businesses. If you run your business well you will find that referrals come naturally. However, there is no harm in encouraging your customers to tell their friends about you. There are several strategies you can use to promote referrals:

- **Offer incentives.** New customers are valuable, in addition to buying your products or services they also may become referrers themselves. So there is something to be said for investing in referrals, a common tactic among sellers of subscriptions like magazine and website publishers. Giving your regular customers 10 per cent discount vouchers that they can pass on to friends is likely to increase referrals;

if you can reward them as well, that is even better. With referrals it is even more important that you deliver a good-quality product or service, nobody wants to lose the trust of their friends by referring them to second-rate businesses.
- **Distribute marketing materials.** Make sure all customers have copies of your marketing materials, even after the deal has been completed. It is worth remembering that one of the primary uses of business cards, brochures, flyers, and freebies such as promotional mugs, is distribution to existing customers. They can use the information themselves or use it to refer your business to a friend.
- **Establish good relations with other businesses.** Find businesses that market a product or service that complements your offering. For example, if you are an architect, you will probably form relationships with construction companies who may refer architectural work to you, possibly in exchange for you recommending their building services to your design clients. A quality offering is crucial here, no matter how close your personal relationship, no-one will risk their own reputation by recommending work to someone who delivers a second-rate product or service.

PUBLIC RELATIONS

Public relations (PR) exists in the no-man's-land between relationship marketing and

 For further information on the value of building business relationships, see Chapter 9.

straightforward advertising. It used to be the exclusive preserve of big businesses, which would employ public relations staff to explain (or, more often, defend) corporate actions and decisions to the public.

Today PR is much more complex. Although it still involves a lot of relationship management with the public as it did originally, it is now more heavily geared to promoting business in the media.

The principle is a good one. Journalists are always on the lookout for a good story, and if you can provide them with a ready-made one in the form of a press release, they may publish it, resulting in 'free' publicity for your business. This can be a hit and miss affair, however, and you will probably need to 'sell' your story to a journalist in order to see it actually in print.

One word of warning. As you have probably guessed, we keep putting the word 'free' in inverted commas for a reason. Although you would not have to pay the media for publishing a story about you, if use a PR agency, you would have to pay them. Be wary of PR agencies that promote themselves as able to 'guarantee' you coverage in a named set of publications. Although the agency may have developed strong relationships with a journalist or editor, most media pride themselves on their independence and rarely give guarantees to any public relations people.

Potentially more costly still, is the fact that PR is not entirely free of risk. Once your story is released to journalists, all kinds of things can happen. Facts can get mixed-up in newspaper stories, you might be portrayed in an unsympathetic light, or your details and web address can be mixed up with a competitor. In short, the media can't always be relied on to do exactly what you want it to do, and whenever you attempt to exploit it to promote your business you are dealing with a form of marketing that is fundamentally beyond your control.

That said, for most businesses PR is a very useful tool, and if it is handled correctly, most of the time everything should go according to plan, though there is no guarantee that your story will be picked up by the media. To improve your chances, try to write a good press release.

Press releases

How you go about distributing your press release depends on your business and the media you are targeting. Printed releases are more hassle for you to print and post out, but they are not as easy to delete as emailed releases. Different journalists will have different preferences. The best way to choose your method of distribution is to ask your recipient what they would prefer. If you run a restaurant for example, check in your local newspapers to see who writes the reviews. When you call the paper, ask for them by name, or ask to speak to the food editor. Once you have got through, briefly explain who you are, that you wish to send them a press release and would they prefer you to email or post it? Keep a note of their

> ❝ You can use PR to get 'free' advertising in the media by sending out a press release. ❞

Key elements of a successful press release

- **An interesting, compelling story.** There is no point putting out a release if you have nothing interesting to say. Despite what you may think from reading newspapers or magazines, journalists do not actively set out to bore their readers. Never try to cram too much into one press release. One release, one story. Unless you have got something very important to say, try to keep your release to around 300-400 words.
- **A human angle.** People like reading about people, so always try to stress the human aspect of any story.

If you are short of something interesting to say you can always manufacture a story: doing some free work for a local charity, for example, allows you to do a bit of good in the community and have something interesting to say in a press release.

- **A quotation.** The journalists that turn your press release into a story (sometimes by juggling the sentences around five minutes before it is published), will always want to quote one of the people involved. It is quite legitimate to write about yourself in the third person in a press release.

- **Statistics.** Where possible include statistics, they can have an important role backing up your claims.
- **Who, what, why, where, when?** These are the key facts that all journalists will want to put in their story. Make sure your press release answers all of them and do not forget to include your contact details. If the journalist wants to check a fact, collect more quotes, or even discuss writing a bigger story or feature about you, they need to know how to get hold of you quickly and easily.

name and preference and make sure all subsequent releases are targeted directly at them, in their preferred manner. Do not be afraid of contacting a journalist directly. They need you as a source for their stories as much as you want them to feature you in their publication. Just make sure that you have a good idea of what your story is about before you call.

The other benefit of contacting a journalist in advance of sending the release is that they are more likely to remember you and read the release once they do receive it. Most journalists receive dozens of press releases every week and yours will have to compete for attention. If you do send your press release by email,

include the text in the body of the email itself and not as an attached file, unless your contact has specifically asked for an attachment. Most sensible internet users are wary about opening email attachments from people they do not know. Press releases tend to be written in two main styles; either mimicking a news story (see overleaf) or as a list of facts, normally presented as an introductory sentence or two followed by a selection of bullet points. There is no right or wrong version, and different journalists on the same publication will have radically different preferences. If you are less confident about writing, just list the facts, include a quotation and let the journalist write the story.

This means the information must not be published before the date. Most media will respect such rules. If a story does not need a 'start date', you can write 'for immediate publication' here.

WHY The text is an upbeat, local business success-story, aimed at this newspaper which is local.

WHEN The release is 'new'. Newspapers like to publish news, which means things that have just happened. If Annette's business had been running for several months, it would not be so newsworthy as the fact that it has just launched.

WHAT Annette explains her offer succinctly.

WHERE The event took place at the arboretum.

WHO Annette provides contact details so that she can be contacted for new quotations, photographs, or further information.

MORE Always leave the door open. By suggesting that she could comment further on any aspect of her subject, Annette is opening herself up for future quotation as an 'expert'. This could be especially useful if the paper were to do a special feature on gardens, for example, as Annette would have a greater chance of ensuring the name of her company is included.

Try to direct the press release at a named reporter or editor in the most appropriate section of the paper.

Make it clear to even the most rushed reporter exactly what they are looking at.

Branding the press release gives a more professional look.

A Jones
Business Editor
Anytown Evening News
Anytown

Press Release

Greenlands
GARDEN DESIGN

● **Embargoed until Monday 10th May**

Business is Blooming in Anytown

Beautifully manicured lawns and soothing, landscaped water features will soon become a regular feature of Anytown gardens, thanks to green-fingered designer Annette Smith.

Annette's new business, Greenlands Garden Design, enjoyed an enthusiastic launch party yesterday beneath the Spring blossoms of Anytown arboretum, amid widespread speculation that her business will soon dominate the garden services sector in Anytown and the surrounding area.

"After conducting some in-depth market research, I saw there was a strong need for high quality, cost effective, design skills with garden owners, professional gardeners and garden centres who could use my services as an add-on to their own offering", explains Annette.

"I've had tremendous feedback and if all goes well in Anytown, we have plans to expand our offer throughout the region", she adds.

Greenlands Garden Design offers a free quotation service and customers are invited to cherry pick from a wide range of design advice and services. "Greenlands is all about beautiful gardens, no matter what their size or their owner's budget. We can do everything from advising on the best shape for a patio and winter bed, to landscaping a garden from scratch and co-ordinating its on-going upkeep," says Annette.

Annette trained at Anytown Horticultural College and worked at Anytown Garden Centre as a garden design adviser before launching out on her own. She received advice from Anytown Business Link and conducted her own market research prior to launch. A selection of before and after photographs can be seen at her website www.greenlandsgardens.co.uk

Annette is always available for comment or advice on any issues concerning horticulture or garden design. For further information or photographs contact:
**Annette Smith, Greenlands Garden Design, Any Street, Anytown, AN1 1AN
Tel: xxxxx xxxxxx www.greenlandsgardens.co.uk**

Marketing Materials

Marketing materials are what you use to promote your business, including brochures, flyers and your website. In this section we will focus on printed materials which, as opposed to online marketing, is still the nuts and bolts of many marketing campaigns.

Printed marketing materials can take a wide variety of formats, from simple A5 flyers to glossy folders and brochures. Using print material might seem a bit old-fashioned in these hi-tech days, but it is so versatile and (relatively) cheap to produce that it is likely to remain a part of small business marketing for a very long time to come. Consider all the things you can do with simple leaflets that promote your business:

- Put them through letterboxes in targeted areas.
- Pay people to hand them out in town centres.
- Send them out with mailing letters and products.
- Leave them in pubs, shops and takeaways (with permission!).
- Use them as 'leave-behinds' after meetings with clients.
- Send them out as part of a 'press pack' with your press releases.

You can have thousands of leaflets and basic brochures printed for just a few hundred pounds. Given the wide range of uses you can then put them to, it can be a very cost-effective means of advertising.

A good designer will advise you on the type of leaflet or brochure that is right for you. You might want something large and glossy, in which case, obviously, you will wind up paying a bit more in print and design costs. On the other hand, you might get away with an A5 flyer or a bifold or trifold leaflet – a simple piece of printed A4 folded once or twice to provide a miniature brochure with four (bifold) or six (trifold) panels. If you have a decent printer you can even make these at home if you only need a small number.

Another popular and cost effective technique is to invest in a few thousand glossy, high quality A4 folders with an internal pocket. The folder makes a good impression, and the interior pocket can be filled with material to suit the individual client you are giving the package to. Print material can also be adapted to include detachable forms and weird-and-wonderful structures like bangtails and gatefolds, perfect for including in a direct mail package.

The variety of effects that can be achieved with modern materials, printing and die-cutting techniques, is practically limitless. If you can find a good designer and a print firm that is willing to take on unusual jobs, you can produce just about anything from promotional pop-up books to marketing flyers that can be transformed into origami boats or paper planes.

And the material you print on does not have to be paper. There are endless promotional opportunities to be had from mugs, teddy bears, t-shirts, umbrellas, beer mats, shopping bags and so on, the list is endless.

Jargon Buster

Bangtail A detachable extension, with a perforated edge, found on the back of an envelope. It is normally used to contain marketing information or an order form, such as a reply-paid slip.
Gatefold A foldout, especially one that opens to double the page size.

THE BASICS

Before you start getting excited about printing your logo in fifty-foot letters on the side of a hot air balloon, you need to think about some more basic stationery requirements. It is really important to have a business card, and if you use a lot of written correspondence you will need headed-paper, along with compliments slips if you are dispatching products by post. Headed-paper is also a requirement for many wholesale accounts.

It can be very tempting to produce these cheaply at home. However on the whole, unless you are a professional

designer with top-end printing equipment (and a very steady hand with a pair of scissors), doing so will be a false economy; you will just be using up valuable time for mediocre results. If you want a professional look, get a designer to put everything together for you and then employ a printer to produce the goods. When it comes to cards, ensure that the stock used is a minimum weight of 220gsm. Go for 300-400gsm if you can afford it, as a denser, stiffer business card conveys a greater sense of authority and quality than something flimsy. It may seem odd that this kind of thing matters, but you will find that people judge your business (sometimes unconsciously) on small things that are wholly unrelated to the quality of your product or service. We will discuss this concept in greater detail in the section on branding, below.

Do not forget, either, that the trading name of your business must legally appear on your letterheads. If you are a limited company, you must use your full company name and number, along with your VAT number if you have one, in all correspondence. If you are a partnership, all of your partners must be named on the letterhead too.

Jargon Buster

Paper stock The type of card or paper. This may be coated or uncoated, matt or glossy and of a greater or lesser degree of quality. Individual stocks may also be produced in different weights.

CALL THE PROFESSIONALS

You may have all the skills and equipment you need to produce your own marketing materials. This includes:

- Good graphic design.
- Clear, grammatical and correctly-spelt copy (text).
- A good quality printer for your computer.

It is pretty unlikely that you will have this combination of skills and equipment, unless the business you are setting up is itself design-oriented. Even then, most specialist designers contract out writing and printing work. Having other professionals work on the project for you delivers double value: not only do you get marketing materials that are expertly created and produced, you also get an objective view of your business. Sometimes it takes somebody looking in from the outside to see the real benefits of your offering clearly and to produce marketing materials that communicate these benefits in a way that really hits home. The three major professional skills involved in producing marketing materials are design, copywriting and printing.

Take extra care when using designers from different cultures. They can have radically alternative views on what constitutes attractive design, and a design that seems appealing to an Indian or a Russian may look 'wrong' to British eyes.

DESIGN

It is important that your marketing materials make a strong visual impact. First impressions are really important,

(you don't want to lose a customer before they have even tried your product or service) and the 'look' of your business can make a massive difference to your customers' perceptions of it.

There are plenty of graphic designers available. You need to choose one that:

- Has a good portfolio that shows they can do the job to a good standard.
- Fits your budget.
- Understands your business.

Not all designers are equally good, and finding a skilled one is not always easy. Anyone with even basic skills can set up as a designer (a problem we will come across when we discuss website development in the next chapter), so it is unwise to take anyone on without having a careful look at their work. All reputable graphic designers will have a portfolio of work that you can examine. Remember that the material you see in a designer's portfolio is the best he or she can do.

Ensure you talk to the person who will be doing the work. There is an unfortunate (and growing) tendency for individuals in the UK and USA to launch 'design' companies and farm out all the work to cheap providers in Russia, India and the Far East. Establish early on exactly who will be doing your work, and make sure you have a detailed conversation with that individual about your specific needs.

Getting the quality and the cultural aspect right is crucial to a good relationship with a designer. Although very few people can produce really good graphic design, most of us can tell the difference between good design and bad design when we see it. As long as you remember to look at portfolios and have those all-important telephone conversations (or, even better, face-to-face meetings) you should be OK. Remember, too, that you tend to get what you pay for. Finding a designer that fits your price-range is not always easy, because skilled designers are very much in demand and can set their rates quite high. By all means shop around, but remember that it is worth spending a bit extra for a really good look and feel for your marketing materials.

A good designer will work very hard to understand your business. In fact, you should be wary of one who does not ask questions about what you are trying to achieve and the nature and tastes of your target market. Giving your designer the information he or she needs to do a good job on your design project is known as 'briefing'. Ideally you should give your chosen designer a written brief and follow-up with a conversation to address any questions. Your brief should be as detailed and concrete as possible, including information about:

- Your product, including pricing.
- The market you are aiming at.
- Your brand values (see overleaf).

Most designers, once they have grasped the brief, will produce a few draft designs for you to choose from. A really good designer will try to consult with you at every stage, getting a sense of what you like and making amendments to your suggestions.

It is very important to know your own mind before you start dealing with a designer. It will be a waste of time, not to mention a waste of your money, if the designer produces a series of drafts that you hate. Make sure you tell your designer what you are looking for. If you are not entirely sure, define what you don't want and ask your designer to discuss various options with you before putting pen to paper. Another good tactic is to collect any designs and marketing materials that you like. This will help establish your preferences in your own mind and gives the designer a base to work from.

> ❝ Although very few people can produce really good graphic design, most of us can tell the difference between good design and bad design when we see it. ❞

 For further information on how to find a designer and how to brief them, see the Chartered Society of Designers' website, www.csd.org.uk

Once you have taken the time and trouble to find a good designer, listen to the advice he or she gives you. Many new businesses (and a few established ones) get very fussy about trivial points like making logos and telephone numbers as big as possible. Go with your designer's advice on points like this. An experienced professional will know what works.

A final word of warning: if you are after an excellent result on a limited budget, it can be tempting to present a project to a number of designers on a speculative basis. This is a situation in which you approach a designer for draft work on the basis that you will accept and pay for it only if you like it. Many designers see this kind of approach as exploitative and some, such as those who are members of the Chartered Society of Designers, sign up to a protocol where they all refuse to do 'free pitches'. In addition, you will probably get a better job from a designer when you promise to pay. You cannot expect the best results for no money.

Copywriting

'Copy' is the industry term for text. It covers all the writing on your website and marketing materials. A copywriter is a professional who has the skills that are needed to create specialist text, which may include sales, marketing or other information.

If you are good at writing you could well handle your own copy. Bear in mind, however, that to write copy that really works you need to be able to write English that is:

 Note that copywriting has nothing to do with copyright, the law covering the ownership of creative works.

- Grammatically perfect.
- Free of spelling errors.
- Clear, precise and engaging.

This means avoiding clumsy constructions and pointless words, and staying away from overused phrases and jargon. A good copywriter will do this instinctively, improving the chances your product or service has in the marketplace.

A copywriter will also understand how to use copy to sell things. The art of copywriting is too complicated to examine in detail here, so if you decide to write your own, it is worth doing a little research and reading some books on the subject. Among the best on the market are *The Copywriter's Handbook* by Robert Bly, *Ogilvy on Advertising* by David Ogilvy and *Freelance Copywriting* by Diana Wimbs. As its title suggests, the third book is as much about the business of working as a copywriter as it is about writing copy, but it still contains a great deal of useful advice for business owners interested in writing their own sales material.

You and your brand

Branding is for too important to be left to big businesses and their advertising agencies to worry about. And although branding is mostly common sense, every business, large and small, needs to think about it.

Branding is as important to small businesses as it is to large ones. It is often the difference between survival and failure, and frequently creates the difference between massive success and average performance. Your brand is the sum of the perceptions that people have about your business, and the way you present your business to the world. It is, if you like, your business's 'personality'.

All brands are associated with brand values, the particular traits and characteristics that people associate with products and services. Companies that take branding seriously think carefully about the values they would like their customers to associate with their brands, and actively promote them. You will find that when things go wrong with your product or service, a strong brand can limit the damage to your reputation. A good way to get your head around the idea of branding is to think of concrete examples.

Companies and products with a strong brand

- **Apple.** Apple enjoyed strong brand loyalty with its computers, however, this has been well surpassed by the subsequent success of iPod and iTunes. These are a fantastic example of how innovation and design have merged to create a global superbrand.
- **Dyson.** An accepted world leader in vacuum cleaner technology, Dyson promotes efficiency and attractive design, qualities that a strong and growing customer-base sees echoed in its products.
- **Virgin.** A brand that was born for a mail order record retailer and has since been applied to a range of franchises including air travel, mobile communications and music. The Virgin brand works across all sectors and despite the odd set-back, is consistently perceived as championing the case for consumers.

> **❝** Your brand is the sum of the perceptions that people have about your business, and the way you present your business to the world. **❞**

MANAGING YOUR BRAND

When you launch your business, think carefully about the values you wish people to associate with it. For example, as a specialist jewellery courier you would probably want customers to think in terms of reliability, secure handling, cost-effectiveness and speed. Doing your best to make your company reflect those values is good for business on three levels:

- If the brand values are reflected in your advertising, you are more likely to win new customers.
- Repeat business is a fundamental requirement for most businesses today. A trusted brand built on a solid reputation will encourage customers to keep coming back.
- A strong brand generates referrals.

Branding is about understanding the importance of perceptions and the difference they make to people's buying decisions. You can be very good at what you do, but if you ignore the importance of building your brand you will fail to capitalise on what could be your greatest asset, your reputation.

Four strategies for promoting your brand

- **Live your brand.** This may seem obvious, but the best way to build a strong brand is to do a good job. Regardless of how much money you spend on promoting your speed, reliability and cost-effectiveness, if your service is actually slow, hit-and-miss and overpriced, word will soon get round!
- **Talk to the pros.** We have already discussed the benefits of working with designers and copywriters. When you are working on your brochures, leaflets and advertisements with them, explain what brand values

you have in mind. They can use tried-and-tested techniques to incorporate them into their work: for example, designers can use people's subconscious reactions to colour to emphasise a particular brand value.

- **Promote values internally as well as externally.** If you have employees, make sure they are aware of the importance of your brand and its values. Reinforce them constantly, even to the extent of being obsessive. Coach and encourage your staff to embrace those brand

values and live up to them every minute they are working for you.

- **Sell around your brand.** If you decide to put together a special offer or an advertising campaign to win new business, consider building it around your brand. The specialist jewellery courier could promote his speed brand value by emphasising the business's seven-day, 24-hour service. Alternatively, he could promote his secure handling value by producing an advertisement containing images of the valuable products that he specialises in.

❝ Companies that take branding seriously think carefully about the values they would like their customers to associate with their brands, and actively promote them. **❞**

NAMING YOUR BUSINESS

The name of your business is very important. It's an integral part of your brand. Combine a strong brand with a business name that is chosen with effort and planning, and you will significantly out perform the thousands of businesses that don't appreciate its importance.

Ideally your business name should tell people what you do, or if it doesn't, have a strapline that adds an important message and makes you stand apart from your competitors.

'Database Wizards' with the strapline 'Customised databases for small businesses' is more likely to generate enquiries from its targeted customer base than a generic name like King Solutions.

It is also worth considering emotive words that can manage perceptions. For example Sunrise, BlueWater and Horizon, give the impression of something fresh or new, while Express, Sprint and Jet suggest to customers that speed is important and they are likely to get a quick turnaround.

When you come to choosing a name for your business, make a list of potential words and phrases, brainstorm ideas with friends, family and potential customers and then survey the results. It's far better to get negative feedback early on, than wait until your stationery and business cards have all been printed and your name has been painted above the door.

Don't despair if, after all of your brainstorming attempts, you have still not come up with a name that you like. Many design agencies, copywriters and marketing agencies specialise in what they call 'name generation'. The amount of time they spend on this will be dictated by your budget, but most creatives take the process of name generation very seriously and will do a great deal of research in order to find a name that has a good reason for being your company's name.

When researching possible names for your company, it is well worth researching domain names at the same time. If you plan to have a website, it makes sense for the domain name to be as close to your business name as possible. If no domains are available for the specific name you had in mind, then think again.

❝ If all goes according to plan, your business is going to be around for a long time. Give it the best possible chance with a smart logo that reflects your brand values. ❞

All limited companies must register with Companies House and no two companies within the same sector are allowed to have the same name. So, in addition to thinking about whether your proposed business name already exists as a domain, you will also need to check whether it is available at Companies House. Although the same rules do not exist for sole traders and partnerships

131

(as these businesses do not need to register with Companies House), it will not help your business if it shares a name, or a similar name, with a competitor.

Finally invest in a professionally designed logo. If all goes according to plan, your business is going to be around for a long time. Give it the best possible chance with a smart logo that reflects your brand values. If your budget is particularly tight you can use logo design software or alternatively research the many design services on the internet. But don't dismiss your local network, this is a great opportunity to start building your contacts. Ask around for recommendations, good local freelance designers can be very competitive and many of them offer package deals for both logos and stationery.

❝ When researching possible names for your company, it is well worth researching domain names at the same time. ❞

Advertising

What is the best way to advertise your business? How effective will it be? What techniques should you use? To conclude this chapter, we will explore the options available to you in advertising.

We have already discussed several traditional methods of promotion, and we are going to take a look at some more hi-tech techniques in the next chapter. However, it is well worth taking a detailed look at how to put together a traditional print advertisement such as one that a small business would typically run in a local newspaper, trade magazine or a directory such as the *Yellow Pages*.

This type of advertisement will generally be text-based, perhaps incorporating some imagery. Once again, it can be useful to hire professionals to design and write your advertisement for you.

If, however, you are simply thinking about advertising your services in a local paper, you probably will not want to go to that kind of expense. Fortunately, putting together a basic print advertisement is not that complicated. There is even a formula you can follow.

A.I.D.A.

Follow the A.I.D.A. formula and you will not go far wrong. It stands for:

- **Attention.** Use headlines to grab attention and highlight a key benefit.
- **Interest.** Develop the headline, filling in details of your offer.
- **Desire.** Explain how your offer can make life or business more fun, profitable, or easier.
- **Action.** Invite customers to contact you with a telephone number, web address, or both.

Most print advertisements can be analysed as an A.I.D.A. structure, whether they are promoting lawn mowers in a local paper, or BMWs in a glossy magazine.

However, the structure is most obvious at the budget end of the advertising marketing.

A few things to bear in mind when you are creating short advertisements include:

- Focus on benefits, benefits, benefits. What is the benefit to the customer? What will your product or service do for them?
- Make sure your writing and design is accurate. If you make a spelling mistake, you will soon hear about it!
- In advertising, less is more: use a few words and focus on a single major benefit of your product or service, with maybe one minor benefit (say, a price reduction).

Here are a selection of real print advertisements.

They have been annotated to illustrate how the A.I.D.A. formula works in practice.

Attention. Use headlines to grab attention and highlight a key benefit.

Desire. Explain how your offer can save your customers time or money, make their businesses more profitable, or their lives easier or more fun.

Interest. Develop the headline, filling in details of your offer.

Action. Invite customers to contact you with a telephone number, web address, or both.

SPECIAL MEMBERS' OFFER

To order, call 01903 828557 or email mailorder@lbsltd.co.uk and quote code PREPUBW906

Brand new –
Which? essential guides
Pre-publication offer, £1 off rrp plus free p&p

This month we're celebrating the launch of two new 'Which? essential guides'– Renting and Letting and What to do When Someone Dies. Containing all the thorough research and independent advice you'd expect from Which?, these essential guides are practical, easy-to-use,

feature lots of pull-out tips, helpful websites and useful contacts – and they cover all the recent legislation changes. The books will be in the shops from mid-September but Which? members can buy copies early for the special price of £9.99 (usual rrp £10.99) plus free p&p.

Renting and Letting
Kate Faulkner (ISBN: 978-1-84490-029-9)
224pp

A practical guide for anyone letting out or renting property. Covering student accommodation, business lets, second homes and holiday flats, this guide points out the pitfalls to avoid as well as suggests the ways to increase your chance of success. Provides up-to-date advice and everything you need to know about the financial and legal practicalities.

What to do When Someone Dies
Paul Harris (ISBN: 978-1-84490-028-2)
224pp

An invaluable handbook dealing with the practical arrangements surrounding bereavement. From registering a death to administering an estate, this guide provides clear, easy-to-follow advice and presents the options available. Offers advice on how long things take, practical considerations and expenses you are likely to incur.

INDEPENDENT EXPERT ADVICE YOU CAN TRUST

❝ It can be useful to hire professionals to design and write your advertisement for you. ❞

Targeting and testing

It is possible to use audience targeting and testing with print advertisements in the same way that you would with direct marketing, although the results are not likely to be quite as precise.

If you are serving a particular geographical area you can place your advertisements in the local paper or *Yellow Pages*. If you are targeting a specific market, it may be more beneficial to consider specialist media, such as business and hobby magazines. Just about every trade and subject you can imagine has its own journal or magazine, often with very competitive advertising rates. Depending on your experience or the uniqueness of your offer, an alternative approach is to write an article. Trade and hobby magazines are always on the lookout for contributors. A well-written article can help establish you as an expert and get coverage for free.

An advertisement designed for newspapers and magazines can also be adapted or expanded for use in your other marketing materials, such as leaflets, brochures and flyers.

You can try to measure the effectiveness of your advertisement by seeing if sales enquiries increase after you have run it. However, this is often not a very accurate measurement. If you have run an advertisement in five different newspapers, or split-tested three different advertisements against each other, you want to know which one has generated the most sales. You can do this by offering a promotion, such as a small discount on your prices in the advertisement, that customers can access by quoting a simple promotional code when they contact you. This can be, for example, the name of the paper in which they saw the advertisement. That may cost you a little extra, but it will allow you to pinpoint reasonably which of your advertising strategies have been most successful; information you can use to your advantage the next time you run an advertising campaign.

❝ An advertisement designed for newspapers and magazines can also be adapted or expanded for use in your other marketing materials, such as leaflets, brochures and flyers. ❞

The Advertising Standards Authority (ASA) is the independent organisation set up by the advertising industry to police rules set out in the advertising codes. Non-broadcast advertising is governed by the CAP Code. For further information on the ASA and the advertising codes see, www.asa.org.uk

Online business

It is impossible to ignore the internet. Whatever business you are thinking of starting, if you deal with customers there is a benefit to be had from a presence on the web. The internet not only allows you to reach a wider audience faster than would have been dreamed of just a few years ago, it also allows you to automate many aspects of your business.

Online opportunities

You can divide the world into three groups: those who do not understand the internet, those who take it for granted, and a broad middle group that uses it but does not quite appreciate its full potential.

You can't afford to ignore the internet. Take a moment to consider the statistics:

- **FACT 1** Online sales will reach £40 billion this year, totalling 15 per cent of all UK retail sales.
- **FACT 2** 8m households in the UK spend on average two hours a day shopping online. They part with about 10 per cent of their annual shopping bill, about £980 a year.
- **FACT 3** Britons spend more money online than their European counterparts. Total European spending on the internet hit £70 billion in 2007.
- **FACT 4** 77 per cent of business -to-business companies regard the primary purpose of a website to be the 'source of company and product/service information'.

Less than 10 years ago our day-to-day communications were based on the telephone, fax machine and mail. Global business was the preserve of corporate giants, research took place in reference libraries, and advertising and routes to market were dominated by *Yellow Pages*, list brokers and printed media.

However, for all the positive changes that the internet has brought to the way we do business, it can also harm our businesses when not used properly. Here are four examples:

- A poorly-designed or confusing website could damage your brand: customers may assume that if you cannot run a decent website, your products or services might not be up to much either.

Jargon Buster

Application A piece of computer software that allows you perform a specific task, such as word-processing. In casual conversation it's often used interchangeably with 'program'.

Ecommerce The buying and selling of products and services using the internet to manage the whole sales process.

" The internet allows you access to a much broader market than you might otherwise have had. "

- People are used to immediate responses. If you do not reply to an email enquiry, users begin to question your efficiency.
- If you do not pay enough attention to security you can lose a lot of time or money as a result of virus infection or identity theft.
- You can create a fantastic website, but unless visitors find you, enjoy their experience and want to buy your service or product, it will not do you much good.

A WIDER AUDIENCE

The internet allows you access to a much broader market than you might otherwise have had. This benefit is obvious for self-employed service providers like consultants, writers and designers, who can send their work via email to clients anywhere in the world. But it is also very true for many traditional businesses, now that increasing numbers of people go online to buy or research goods and services in their local areas.

As well as a worldwide audience, the internet also offers businesses the opportunity to interact with clients like never before, such as through blogs and online forums. Of course, customer interaction has always taken place: one of the secrets of building a successful business has always been to develop relationships with your customers.

Case Study **Tim**

Tim clears blocked sewers and drains. He has a van and a wide variety of equipment to help him fix blockages in remote and inaccessible pipes. Tim's a great believer in technology – he was one of the first in his region to use CCTV and infra-red technologies, to diagnose waste pipe problems remotely. He decides to set up a website to supplement his existing marketing effort, which up until now has comprised a weekly advert in the local paper and a display listing in his local telephone directory.

Tim knows that he does not need a glamorous website, (he is not in a glamorous business), but he does understand that his website needs to be clear, usable and easy to find. After trawling the web, he found some ready-made templates that were ideal. He then designed it himself, having made the most of the free training available on websites like www.webmonkey.com and www.w3c.org. He also pays some attention to search engine optimisation (a subject we'll look at in some detail later in the chapter), and takes some time to register his new website with online business directories.

After a few weeks Tim finds that he is getting more enquiries, many from outside his usual area of operations. Some offers of work come from so far away that he is not able to take them on. However, this convinces him that there is a wide market for his type of service, and opens up the possibility of expanding his business or developing a franchise.

Previously, however, those relationships were built over the telephone, in meetings or on your business premises. The internet brings the power to make (and break) customer relationships right to your desk.

Crucially, blogs, forums and user reviews also allow your customers to talk to each other. One of the most valued commodities on the web is informed opinion. Chances are that you have used such resources to research a particular product or service before making a purchase. You might well consult consumer sites such as www.which.co.uk and www.tripadvisor.co.uk, but you will also find fascinating insights in the hundreds of thousands of forums and blogs in which just about any product or service you can imagine is discussed.

> **❝ Since the early days of the internet, customers have come to expect more from online businesses. ❞**

Search engine websites like Google recognise the value of informed opinion to their users, which seems to be why they usually give relevant forums and blogs high positions within search results.

Since the early days of the internet, customers have come to expect more from online businesses. Even though it is easier to visit a site on the internet than visit the High Street, it is also easy for a customer to click away from a website and never return. For a site to work today it has to address the real 'what's in it for me' questions that customers constantly ask themselves as they surf the web. Why should they spend any time on your site? More importantly why should they return or recommend it to others?

You need to put yourself in the visitor's position and ask yourself those questions. What is in it for them? If you were visiting a site like yours, what would you like to see?

A good place to start is with good content. That does not mean sales spiel, it means information that your customers would benefit from. This is usually your knowledge and experience of your particular field of business. Depending on your skills, this can come in the form of articles, blogs, video presentations or podcasts.

Search engines favour sites that have good quality content. Websites that contain a good deal of interesting, free information are likely to be more popular with visitors. Offering a content-rich site is now considered to be the norm for online traders. A business website that simply promotes your services or sells your product, (in other words, acts purely as a medium for advertising and sales), is less likely to be popular with both human readers and search engines, and, consequently, will receive fewer visitors.

BUSINESS MADE EASY

The internet does not actually make business easy, but it can make many aspects of it easier and more automatic than they used to be.

Say you wanted to buy a new toaster in 1990. Your choice was limited to those in stock at retailers within a reasonable distance of your home. Alternatively, you could get hold of a catalogue and buy one by mail order. Both of these processes took time. Today you can visit an ecommerce site and complete the whole transaction in ten minutes. If you compare prices between sites and read some reviews, you might take as long as if you had driven to the High Street, but in most cases you will get a better deal online, and you will probably receive your purchases almost as quickly, with an increasing number of online retailers offering next day delivery.

Making the most of the internet allows you to:

- Sell your product or service to anyone, anywhere in the world.
- Save time and money sourcing products, materials and subcontractors.
- Change your pricing and offer in moments.
- Offer different prices to customers, for example trade customers compared to consumers, and, for international trade, prices in local currencies.

How to create a content-rich website

- Offer a series of online articles about your area of expertise.
- Write a blog about your business, offering tips and advice to customers and addressing common problems. This is a great way of giving your business a human face (which is always appealing).
- Remember to keep it up to date, though, if customers see you are not looking after your online presence, they will wonder how well you will look after them.
- Allow customers to post online reviews of products. This is a great way of generating valuable content for your site for free.
- If you sell business-to-business, allow customers to leave a signature (name and website) under their testimonial. This will encourage people to leave positive comments; everybody likes a free link to their own sites.

- Take credit card payments, and if you use a service like Nochex or PayPal, you do not even need a merchant account with your bank.
- Liaise closely with your delivery contractor, tracking shipments in real time from your business to your customer's front door.

The internet is also a tremendous information source. You can conduct market research, find out about potential suppliers, check legal and tax regulations and seek advice from other self-employed people. Tasks that would have taken hours or days just a few years ago can now be accomplished in a fraction of that time.

Online threats

As we have seen in the previous section, the internet offers great opportunities to the self-employed. However, there are also a number of dangers you need to be aware of when starting a website or 'dotcom' business.

Spam, computer viruses, spyware and phishing, can all cause a range of problems for your business, from affecting your computer's performance to stealing your financial details.

SPAM

Spam has become a universal problem for most users of the internet, and for businesses the threat is even more serious. If you have had an email account for any length of time you have almost certainly received some spam. These are unsolicited emails offering to sell you products, often of an inappropriate and occasionally illegal nature. Even at its most innocent, sorting out genuine emails from spam is time-consuming. Your time is valuable, so reducing or cutting out spam will be worth the effort in the long run.

Spammers (the criminals who send spam) have an increasingly difficult job, mostly because 'anti-spam' software is becoming more sophisticated. Most email accounts come with built-in spam filtering, which should remove a large proportion of the junk emails that arrive in your inbox. If you have a reputable internet service provider or webhost, much of the spam that would otherwise come your way should be stopped before it even reaches your computer. However, some will still get through. It is vitally important that you do not download or run any files that are attached to incoming spam emails, they may contain viruses or spyware that could damage your computer or steal information from you. If it is obviously spam, (a good way to check is via the subject line), do not open it. Opening emails can also alert the sender that yours is a 'live' email account belonging to someone who opens unsolicited emails, thereby inviting even more spam your way.

There are a number of tactics, outlined in the box opposite, that you can use to manage or reduce the amount of spam you receive.

When you are looking for a solution to your spam problem you need to strike a balance between keeping out the spam emails and letting through the genuine ones. In the same way that some spam will inevitably get through, some legitimate

❝ Your time is valuable, so reducing or cutting out spam will be worth the effort in the long run. ❞

emails (from new customers, perhaps) may be blocked. For this reason, it is a good idea to open your 'junk email' folder regularly, just to make sure a genuine email hasn't been consigned to the dustbin. If you find any genuine emails in there make sure you mark them as 'not spam' so you don't get a repeat problem.

VIRUSES

The term 'virus' is very broad and applies to a wide range of malicious files that can damage your computer in different ways. Viruses are not 'natural' illnesses that affect your computer, but are created by people who wish to cause harm or chaos to other people's computers, websites or networks. In general, a computer virus can be described as a small program that spreads from computer to computer, replicating itself. It often does some form of damage, ranging from trivial to severe. Among computer specialists you may hear terms like 'malware' and 'badware' used to cover classic viruses as well as other non-virus nasties such as worms and trojans. For the purposes of this section, we will use the word virus as an umbrella to cover all of them. The results of such threats can include:

- The contents of your computer's memory, (including your documents, emails and customer records) being damaged or deleted.
- Your computer being used as a 'zombie' to send spam email to other computers, resulting in a dramatic slowdown of performance.

How to control spam

- Use a web-based email address from a provider such as MSN or Googlemail. These companies typically have very advanced spam filters in place. You can even set up your "official" website address (yourname@yourwebsite.com) to redirect to a web-based account.
- Create additional email accounts to sign up for any free services, offers, prize draws or anything that is outside your core business interests.
- Create rules within Outlook or your email program to automatically forward dubious emails to a spam folder. When you are setting up the rule, you can add unlimited number of banned words to be checked for in the subject line or even the message.
- Buy third party anti-spam software or hardware. Appropriate software has been around for a long while, and comes built in to most popular email applications such as Outlook. However, there is no harm in having an extra layer. Hardware spam solutions such as Spamcube are growing in popularity and are well worth looking at if you have a serious spam problem.
- Do not put your email address on your website, use email forms instead so that messages are automatically forwarded to you. Your web designer will be able to help you set these up. Spammers have programs that automatically 'harvest' email addresses from business websites. Giving a spammer a business email address is doubly dangerous: in addition to sending you spam, he might also use your address to 'mask' his spam emails, making it appear that his spam is coming from you. This can result in your website getting blacklisted by spam filters, meaning legitimate emails that you send may be blocked.

143

- Your contacts' email addresses being harvested from your address book and used by spammers.
- Your credit card or personal details being stolen.

We have already said it is important to not download or open email attachments from people you do not know. It is equally important to take care before opening attachments from known contacts. It is possible for criminals to 'hijack' email addresses and make it appear that an email is from a trusted friend or colleague. If the message in an email seems odd or uncharacteristic, get in touch with the sender to make sure the email is legitimately from them before opening.

The world's first internet-level antivirus software was launched by the British company, MessageLabs in 1999. Today, there are plenty of solutions on the market, some free of charge, and most of them do an excellent job of keeping viruses out. Good antivirus software will identify and neutralise viruses before they affect you, and can be set to scan your system regularly for any problems already present. To keep your antivirus database up to date, it is useful to accept the automatic update option that all the major brands offer.

❝ Good antivirus software will identify and neutralise viruses before they affect you, and can be set to scan your system regularly for any problems already present. ❞

Jargon Buster

Worm A program that replicates itself over a computer network and usually performs malicious actions.

Trojan Horse Also known just as a Trojan, this is a destructive program that masquerades as a benign application. Unlike viruses, they do not replicate themselves.

Web-based email services such as MSN and Googlemail are also useful in combating viruses: they have built-in, constantly-updated antivirus software solutions that continuously check all emails and attachments, free of charge. Most computers these days come with a built-in 'firewall', a program that prevents other programs and online intruders accessing bits of your computer's memory you don't want them to.

SPYWARE

A growing problem for many users of Windows computers is a gradual loss of performance. In addition to the build up of temporary files that Windows automatically generates, an increasing problem is caused by spyware and adware. It is interesting to note that users of alternative web browsers, (such as Mozilla's Firefox) and alternative operating systems (such as Apple's Mac OS X or Linux) are generally not affected by spyware or other viruses at all.

Spyware tracks your online activity and transmits the details back to third parties who use it for commercial purposes. At its worst, Spyware passes itself off as another program, installs itself and then often sends 'request payment' messages to your PC.

Spyware is typically installed onto your system as you surf the net, visit sites and download free trials. Typical sources include instant messaging, popular download management programs, online gaming and adult sites. The latest delivery methods require no permission or interaction with users at all. Microsoft has taken steps to remedy this problem in the latest release of Windows – Windows Vista – but it remains a threat to machines running older operating systems.

Again, a good antivirus application should be able to root out spyware. There are also a number of free spyware scanners available online, like Spybot and Ad-aware.

Other threats

The internet is evolving all the time, and it is useful to stay abreast of new threats that emerge. Two common threats are:

- **Phishing.** This is where criminals obtain passwords, credit card information and other personal details by disguising their websites as respectable and well-known businesses (usually banks), or by contacting internet users by email pretending to be from their bank.
- **Email scams.** Fraudulent email messages that offer large rewards for helping the sender transfer money or access a bank account. The scam usually involves its victims having to hand over some of their own money, after which the criminal behind the whole thing disappears.

How to establish credibility and create a 'safe' website

- Include your full contact details, your full business name, address, telephone number and company number if you are registered as a limited company.
- Use a widely-known and trusted payment gateway such as PayPal or Nochex.
- Include a privacy policy and a set of terms and conditions on a page of your site, linked from every other main page. You can find pro forma policies and terms and conditions on the web. If in doubt, discuss it with a solicitor.
- Offer a money-back guarantee. Explain the details in your terms and conditions.
- Establish a website that is smooth and professional. If your website is unattractive, shoddy and confusing your customers will wonder how safe their credit card details are with you. We will look in more detail at good design and building trust in the next section.

Clearly, if your business is going to require you to spend a lot of time online it is worth familiarising yourself with these threats in more detail, to protect yourself and your customers. Remember that your customers will also have heard about the threats presented by viruses, spam, phishing and the like. If you are planning to sell products or take payments for services online, it is important you set customers' minds at rest by portraying yourself as a credible and trustworthy business.

BACK-UP!

As long as you take the appropriate precautions, it is less likely that your business will suffer because of external threats from the internet. However, it is better to be safe than sorry. You should make sure that any important data (such as customer lists, order numbers and accounts) are protected against disaster. As well as keeping important files on your main computer, you should do at least two of the following:

- Set up an automatic back-up of your data to a secondary drive or other device.
- Print out records so you have a paper copy.
- Upload records to a remote web server, or email them to yourself using a web-based email account that will keep attachments stored permanently.

Backing-up your data in this way ensures that if the worst happens and your computer stops functioning, whether from a virus attack or hardware failure, you will not lose any information that is vital to the running of your business.

Another good way of keeping your data secure from corruption is to partition your hard drive and save your documents in a different partition from your operating system. You should be able to find easy instructions on partitioning in your computer's help files, although this method of back-up is not often required if you follow the above steps.

Jargon Buster

WYSIWYG An acronym that stands for what you see is what you get. It is normally applied to editing programs that show you what your changes look like on screen.

Payment gateway A third party web based business that takes payments on your behalf, saving you the hassle of getting a credit card merchant account with a bank.

Secondary drive A spare hard disk drive that can be attached to your computer via USB or FireWire cables and used as backup storage.

Antivirus and security software

www.freebielist.com/antivirus.htm Index of free antivirus and antispyware downloads. **Free.grisoft.com** Free anitvirus and antispyware software. **www.lavasoft.com** Free antispyware and anti-adware.

There are several established online security software manufacturers that offer continuously updated, comprehensive, security products for home-users, small businesses and larger businesses. These include: antivirus, antispam, adware or pop-up blockers, firewall and encryption services.

The web addresses of the main providers are:

www.kapersky.com
www.mcafee.com
www.messagelabs.com
www.microsoft.com
www.sophos.com
www.symantec.com

Your website

It is an unusual business that does not have its own website these days. If you do not have one, you risk being left behind. Getting your business online does not need to be difficult or expensive, as long as you approach it in the right way.

When it comes to creating a website, you have four choices:

- Use ready-made templates from a web hosting company that allow you to create and update your own website without programming skills. These include a built-in Content Management System. This means you do not need technical know-how to create the site or keep the content up-to-date.
- Invest in a web-building program like Dreamweaver that has a WYSIWYG editor. You can either edit one of their templates or customise one of the thousands that are available on the internet. You simply drag and drop elements such as graphics and text boxes into position on a blank page and the application generates the code automatically.
- Employ a web designer to create a site for you.
- Create your own website from scratch using a simple text editor and HTML coding skills.

THE DIY OPTION

You should not dismiss the DIY option out of hand, even if your knowledge of computers is limited. Although it can be

" Although it can be time-consuming, creating a website is relatively easy once you have mastered a few basic skills. "

time-consuming, creating a website is relatively easy once you have mastered a few basic skills. Building your own site has a number of benefits. Not only will you save cash, you will pick up some useful experience and have a website that you understand how to change and update quickly and easily.

The basic technology used to create websites is Hypertext Mark-Up Language, or HTML. You may also come across acronyms like SHTML, XHTML, DHTML and XML which all refer to the same core technology. Writing your own code can be useful and will allow you to use WYSIWYG applications more effectively, creating websites that are attractive, functional and optimised for search engines.

If you understand the technology you will find it easier to take advantage of some of the cost-saving opportunities the internet offers. Although you should not spend time learning about web technologies at the expense of running your business, it is a good idea to remember that the web can only get more important, so some knowledge of how it works will come in very handy in the future.

Website technologies

- **Cascading Style Sheets (CSS).** These work in conjunction with HTML to govern the appearance and layout of your page. The great strength of CSS is that it saves time when you are editing your site: instead of editing individual elements on every page, you can change the look and feel of the whole site by adjusting to a single stylesheet text file. This would typically cover the fonts, colours and backgrounds used, as well as the positioning of elements such as text and graphics within the page.
- **Scripts.** These are short programs that add interactivity to your site: a classic example of a simple script is a mail form that allows visitors to type in and send a message without opening an email program. A more complex form of scripting works with a database (see below) to run an online shopping cart. There is no need for you spend ages learning the skills and writing the programs for yourself, there are many websites from which you can download scripts free of charge or for a small cost. In addition, most webhosts also offer scripts that you can add to your site very easily. Scripts can be written in a number of different programming languages: Javascript, Perl and PHP are the most common at the moment.
- **Database.** These are computerised systems for storing and organising information. If you are promoting a range of products, or want to have an online shopping cart, a directory of contacts, a catalogue of images, or a bank of articles, it is far more effective for your website to generate pages from a database rather than you laboriously create pages for every item.

You do not need to know anything about how these technologies actually work to launch and run an online business. You can, for example, download a shopping cart system and install it on your website without knowing much about the programming behind it, in much the same way as you can use your washing machine without needing to be an expert on its engineering. However, you will probably find that a partnership with a skilled web developer can be invaluable. As long as you have a broad familiarity with what the technologies are capable of doing, he or she can handle the details.

WEB DESIGN

Web design is an art as well as a science. The best sites have pages that look attractive, as well as fulfilling technical functions. The good news is that you do not necessarily need an artistic streak to do this. It is quite easy and cheap to buy a ready-made template which you can adapt for use as a business website. Online templates usually cost between £25 and £50, and come with all the graphics and fonts you need to create an attractive website. You can edit them with applications like Dreamweaver, or by writing the code by hand if your skills are up to it.

While many templates also require you to have access to an image editing application like Photoshop, template designers will often customise their products for a low price, usually a fraction of what you would pay for an original design.

Using a designer

You may decide that you do not have the time or the talent to build your own website, and that you would prefer the help of a professional web designer. A professionally-designed site is likely to get you more attention within your niche and command more respect from potential customers. If you are working at the higher end of the corporate or consumer markets, a high quality website is a must. Unless you are an experienced designer yourself, a professional will almost certainly make a better job of your website than you will, so it is worth hiring one.

The good news is there is no shortage of choice. Web design has become a very trendy occupation over the past few years with the basic technical (rather than artistic) skills fairly easy to learn. On the downside it is also a business that anyone can set up without formal qualifications, which means there are a lot of providers in the marketplace who may lack experience and knowhow.

How to choose a good web designer

- **Ask around.** If you have contacts with websites they may be able to recommend a designer that fits in with your price range.
- **Look at designers' portfolios.** Many designers have links to their previous projects, live sites that they have created. Is the navigation easy to follow? Are the designs pleasing to the eye? Look at the company's own site. Is it well designed? Ask for a couple of testimonials, previous customers you can ring for feedback.

 Before you publish your website, make sure that you use the code checking function built into most web-builder applications. This will check and suggest any changes to ensure your coding is standards compliant as defined by www.w3c.org. Knowing a bit about HTML and CSS will allow you to use applications like Dreamweaver more effectively, creating websites that are attractive, functional and optimised for search engines.

- Spend time looking at sites in your sector and find ones that you like. Take screen grabs and drop them into a PowerPoint presentation which you can forward to your designers, giving them a clear indication of what you are looking for. Give as detailed a brief as you can, outlining the specific needs of your business and the values behind your brand.

WHAT SHOULD GO ON YOUR WEBSITE?

- Unless you are focusing on a top end market you do not need a website with every bell and whistle. The most important thing is that your site should have a clean, rather than overly busy, design. A simple design will make it easier to navigate.

❝ The web can only get more important, so some knowledge of how it works will come in very handy in the future. ❞

- In terms of budget, if you do not need a product database or a shopping cart you could pay anything from £250 to £1,500 depending on whether you are using a local freelance or a fully fledged design business. Once you add more advanced features you will be looking at a price between £1,000 to £5,000. If your budget is tight your other option is to use an overseas designer though a network like Elance.com. Do your research thoroughly before you decide to choose that route, as it is more difficult to assess and work with providers on the other side of the world.
- Unless you are happy paying your designer to regularly update your site, ask if the design can include a content management system (CMS). This enables you to edit the content of your website using a WYSIWYG editor rather than rely on someone else to make changes. A CMS doesn't need to be expensive: there are free open source products, such as Joomla! and Mambo, which most web designers can incorporate into a design.

❝Unless you are happy paying your designer to regularly update your site, ask if the design can include a content management system. ❞

YOUR WEBSITE'S NAME

Buying a domain (your website's name) is simple, all webhosts sell them and they often come as part of a package that includes hosting. Choosing the right domain name for your website is important. As the online identity of your business, it needs to be professional, reflect your brand and, ideally, assist you in the search engine rankings.

Below are some tips on buying and registering a domain name.

- **Register a proper top level domain.** It is tempting to save money by hosting your website with a free service such as Geocities, or to use the free hosting space available with internet accounts through internet service providers (ISPs) such as AOL. However, these services usually make you include your ISP or webhost's brand name in your domain name. This tends to look a lot less professional than having your own, dedicated .com or .co.uk web address.
- **What to do if the domain name you want is not available.** You are probably best off thinking of an alternative, as only one person or organisation can own a domain name at a time. If www.andyherbertplumbing.com is already taken, you could approach the owner of the domain. It is usually not difficult to find out who it is by using a domain look-up service like

 For a detailed overview of web design, and for further advice and guidance from the Design Council, see www.webdesignforbusiness.org

www.whois.net. The current owner is under no obligation to sell, even if he is not using the domain name, and once he knows that you want it he is likely to ask a high price. However, there is an option with many domain registration sites to put your chosen name on back-order so, if the current owners fail to renew the registration, you are first in line and all you pay is the standard price. It is also worth considering visiting one of the domain trading sites such as www.sedo.co.uk, www.wulux.com or www.afternic.com, where if you cannot find an alternative name, you could use their brokerage service to track down your targeted domain and negotiate on your behalf. In general, the only situation in which a domain name's owner can be forced to give it up is if you can prove he has infringed a trademark. Given that the internet is global, this is a recourse that is generally only open to large businesses with substantial legal resources. You would be far better off going for www.andyherbertplumber.co.uk or www.ahplumber.com. However, you should bear in mind that if there is another business somewhere in the world with a similar domain name to yours, your customer could become confused. Take care not to infringe another business's trademark. You may find yourself having to rebrand your business, or embark on a legal fight.

- **Consider a descriptive name.** It makes a lot of sense to make your domain name reflect your business.

Domain Names

A domain name is the internet address of your website: www.yourwebsite.com or www.yourwebsite.co.uk. It is also sometimes referred to as a URL (short for 'Uniform Resource Locator'). Note that the .com and .uk endings are important. They indicate the top level domain (TLD) of your website, and give visitors a clue about where it is located or what its purpose is. In the UK, companies mainly use .com and .co.uk (a second level domain of .uk), while non-profit organisations use .org or the second level alternative .org.uk. Internet companies often use .net. There are other TLDs, including ones for individual countries (such as .fr for France and .de for Germany) as well as .biz, .name and .info. There are some restrictions on the names you can obtain. You cannot, for example, register a .gov (government) domain name for a private enterprise.

www.andyherbertplumber.com may be more of a mouthful than www.andyherbert.com, but it sums up what you do. It is also useful for search engine optimisation (see page 157). If a visitor to the search engine Google searches for 'plumber', the results will generally give a higher rank to domain names that actually include that search term. If you operate a local business, including your location in your domain name can be beneficial. As an example www.doggrooming-harrogate.co.uk is more likely to be picked up by the search engines when people are looking for dog groomers in Harrogate. Using a brand name that is unrelated to your business can work: it certainly does for www.monster.com (careers), www.bebo.com (social networking) and www.amazon.com (books, DVDs etc.) However, all of these companies have very large marketing budgets which they can use to ensure that their target market understands what the domain name represents. If you do not, it is a good idea to stick to something descriptive.

- **Keep it active.** A domain name is registered for a set period of time, usually two years. When this expires, anyone can buy it. Make sure you renew your domain before this. Companies exist that make their money by buying up expired domains the minute they become available. Expired domains still attract visitors, and the profit lies in redirecting them to other sites, often run by spammers. You probably do not want to wake up one morning and discover that your domain name is now being used for a website that offers pornography or dodgy pharmaceuticals, so keep it registered in your name. A reputable webhost will send you reminder emails when re-registration time comes around but to prevent this from being overlooked, it's worth ticking the option for automatic renewal when you first register.

- **Register alternatives.** Different people or businesses can own different TLDs with the same website name. For example, if you own www.yourwebsite.com, someone else could buy www.yourwebsite.co.uk. If you value your brand, you might consider buying all the major non-national TLDs for your domain name. Not only will this prevent other business from using the same name, if you put a redirect on the alternative TLDs, it will also make sure that you do not lose any traffic. To the same end, it might be worth registering misspellings, so that you also catch many of the potential customers who may have mistyped your domain name.

PLANNING YOUR WEBSITE

Think carefully about how easy your site will be to use and how it will interact with your visitors. One of the main reasons for online businesses losing sales, is when customers find a website confusing or hard to navigate. Follow this seven-step process to make sure that your website is as easy to use as possible:

- **Create a Site Plan.** Before you even think about the visual appearance of your site, draw a simple plan of the site structure. This is called a 'wireframe'. List the main pages (Home, Products, Services, Contact Us and so on) and

> **❝ Give clear directions to your home page. If a visitor has found your site via a search engine, they may not come to the home page first. ❞**

below each main page, list the subpages for each section.

- **Identify a clean look.** Search the internet for design ideas that that you like. Consider sites that sell similar products and services. Take a look at the major template sites. This will also help you identify a logical structure as well as outline ideas for a design.
- **Create a list of items.** Consider features that will make visitors more likely to return or recommend your site to others, such as a contact form, a simple autoresponder to automatically send a reply to any emails received, a 'recommend a friend' script, a list of useful resources, a shopping cart, or a list of Frequently Asked Questions.
- **Employ user-friendly systems.** Take care to ensure your customer's journey through the site from home page to ecommerce page is smooth and natural. Don't forget the basics, such as telling your customers the price of a product before they need to pay for it.
- **Give clear directions to your home page.** If a visitor has found your site via a search engine, they may not come to the home page first. Your navigation should be designed with this in mind, offering visitors clear directions to the main home page at all times.
- **Test the site before it goes live.** Larger organisations will always build in an element of 'user-testing' to their website development process. You can do the same at a fraction of the cost by asking a sample of family and

friends to explore your site, imagining that they are interested in what your business has to offer. Do not talk them through it, just watch as they navigate. If you notice that they are having trouble finding information, or negotiating a process, make a note of it. If they cannot find their way around your site by themselves, other people will not be able to either. The people who help you test your site are also

Useful statistical information about your website

- **Conversion.** The percentage of visitors to your site that convert to paying customers. If the percentage stays very low (say, around one or two per cent, depending on the price of your product and the competition), track your visitors' movements through the site and make changes to see if you can improve things.
- **Average visit time.** The longer visitors stay on your site the more likely they are to return and refer others.
- **Unique visitors.** Review the number of unique and returning visitors you have. This information will tell you if your site is establishing itself. You would expect traffic to increase, but don't let this make you complacent; you will need to work on the site promotion and content constantly.
- **Last page visited.** Is there is a particular page visitors go to and then leave, without making a purchase or exploring any further? If so, go back and experiment with the design, layout and sales copy on your site. One of the great things about websites is that they can be changed very quickly, allowing you to test and refine almost on an hour-by-hour basis.

likely to be more patient than potential customers. Real web users will only tolerate confusion (or slowness) for a few seconds before giving up and looking elsewhere.

- **Monitor your site once it is up and running.** All good webhosting packages allow you to look at the usage statistics of your website. Alternatively you can use Google Analytics free of charge. The information you can gather includes where in the world your visitors come from, which website referred them to you and, if they came to you from a search engine, the words they typed into the search box.

WEB HOSTING

Once your website is designed, it needs somewhere to live. Websites are stored ('hosted') on special computers called 'servers'. When you access a website, your computer sends a request to that site's server over the internet, and the server sends the relevant web pages back.

You do not need to own a web server to run an internet site. Instead, you rent space on a server owned by a web hosting company, which keeps it on their premises and do all the necessary technical work for you. The idea of shared hosting is that your host company keeps your website alongside several others on the same server to save money. If you are running a large or busy website, you may need to rent a whole server to yourself.

Web hosting can be very cheap, just a few pounds per month for a basic package. If you are working with a web design and development company, they should be able to recommend a web host to you, or even host your site on their own servers. However, renting and managing your own web space is very simple. All hosting packages come with a control panel to help you upload files and manage your website easily.

When buying web hosting services, it pays to shop around. Some of the best deals are provided by companies in the United States. Your website can indeed be hosted anywhere in the world, however, if you are aiming at a predominantly British audience you might consider hosting your site in the UK. A UK-hosted site should work slightly faster, especially if you are using memory-intensive features like sound and video. Additionally, if you are running an ecommerce website, or some other reasonably complex setup, the chances are that you will spend a certain amount of time on the telephone to your host's technical department. Call costs and time zone differences can mean it is more convenient, if sometimes a little more expensive, to host your site in the UK.

When you are looking for a web host, you will probably come across the following terms:

- **Web space.** This is the amount of

 For a comprehensive guide to web standards published by the World Wide Web Consortium, including exhaustive glossaries and tutorials for would-be web developers, see www.w3.org

storage space a web hosting package offers, measured in megabytes (Mb). A single megabyte will hold 20-40 average-sized images or around 150,000 words of text. That may sound a lot, but web space gets eaten up pretty quickly once you have uploaded all the necessary bits and pieces to your website, especially if you are including sound and video files. The very cheapest hosting packages usually come with 50Mb of space, and you should treat that as a bare minimum. If you are running an ecommerce site, you will probably need more space to run a product database effectively.

- **Bandwidth allocation.** This is the amount of data that can be transferred to and from your web server in a given period of time, usually a month. Every time you upload (send) material to your web server or a visitor looks at downloads (receives material from it), the server has to do work and consume energy. A bandwidth allocation of 10 gigabytes means that 10,000 megabytes of information can be transferred in any month. That means if you get more than 5,000 visitors a month, you will exceed your bandwidth allocation, in which case your web host will probably charge you a premium rate for the additional amount. They may even insist you upgrade your hosting package. When you start out, this might not be a problem, but as your business grows you may soon find you are busting your bandwidth limits. If you are selling a product online, or

featuring sound or video on your website, you will need quite a high bandwidth allocation.

- **Email addresses.** Most web hosting packages include plenty of email addresses. If you are self-employed, chances are that you will only need one or two. However, if you are running an ecommerce business, using additional addresses for sales, enquiries, support and so on, will make your communications easier to manage.

- **Database.** This may be a list of your products, or the content management system that contains the material that appears on your website. Databases, including the most common type, MySQL, are unlikely to be found on basic hosting packages. If you need one, your web designer or developer should be able to help you choose a hosting package to suit your needs.

- **Guaranteed uptime.** This is the time that your website spends 'up' and is accessible to visitors. Like any piece of equipment, servers need to be maintained and repaired. Sometimes they do go wrong, leaving your website unavailable. Most reputable hosts use several servers to provide back-up if one fails. This makes them very reliable, and many guarantee 99.9 per cent uptime in any one month. Unless you are planning to become a major ecommerce operator, uptime is not something you should worry about too much.

Driving traffic

Internet marketing experts use the term 'traffic' to describe website visitors. If your website is going to be a successful part of your business, you need as much good-quality traffic as possible. In this section we are going to look at some techniques for leading people to your site.

The golden rule of internet marketing is to remember that the web is not just a marketplace, it is a collection of communities. As with a real-life community, you will find that the more you put in, the more you will get out. This does not just mean offering a good product at a good price, it means identifying communities that are a focal point for your customers and other businesses in your field.

Online forums are ideal. Apart from being an excellent way of contacting customers within your target market, most offer a certain amount of free advertising by allowing you to customise your signature strip, (the short section of text that appears automatically at the end of every post you make). A good signature strip should be short; your website address and a sentence or two summarising your business and the main benefit you offer customers. When you sign up to a forum, it is also useful to complete your forum profile page. People who are serious about doing business with you will want to find out more by looking at your profile and website before contacting you.

Blogs are a good example of the community-oriented nature of the internet. If you write a blog to promote your business, you should encourage other members of the web community to come along and add useful comments to it. The best way of doing this is to attract attention by adding constructive or helpful comments to other people's blogs. If you are adding a valuable contribution to someone else's site (and maybe their business), the chances are that they will come and do the same for yours. This kind of activity builds a 'buzz' around your website. You will steadily get more visitors, and if those visitors find your business website useful or interesting, the ones that themselves own blogs or websites may well put a link to your site on theirs. Most blog

> **Remember to complete your profile page when you sign up to a forum. People who want to do business with you may want to find out more by looking at your profile and website before contacting you.**

providers will host your blog on their servers if you wish, though this will be under their domain name, for example, www.yourbusinessblog.blogger.com.

Many providers will also allow you to upload static blog pages to your website, so you can have an address like www.yourbusinesswebsite.com/yourbusinessblog. However, some providers such as the open source WordPress, allow you to upload the blogging software to your web server and blog dynamically, meaning visitor comments and discussion can take place in real time. Some services charge a fee for enhanced membership, which offers additional benefits.

SEARCH ENGINES

Users of the internet find their way around by a number of methods. The most important of these is search engines. People will use a search engine like those operated by Google, Yahoo! and Lycos, and type in keywords or key phrases that describe what they are looking for, such as: 'discount bicycles', 'window cleaners in Bournemouth'. The search engine will present them with a list of relevant web pages, ranked in what it considers to be the order of importance.

The higher your website's ranking in search engine results pages (SERPs), the more traffic you will get. If your site is properly designed and the product or service you are offering is worth having, some of these new visitors will become your customers. So the higher you rank, the more business you get.

Search Engine Optimisation

The fight to get to the top of the SERPs has led to the birth of a whole internet industry: search engine optimisation, or SEO. The rules of SEO are always changing. If a high result is really vital to your business, you should consider hiring a specialist SEO consultancy to help you, there are thousands on the market and pricing is competitive.

If you are going it alone, and for most small businesses, there is no reason why you should not, there are nine basic steps to help you take your website's ranking to a reasonable level. These are based on what seems to work for Google, the most popular of the search engines.

Google and the other engines base their searches on complex mathematical formulae known as 'search algorithms'. They keep the exact details of these algorithms secret to prevent unscrupulous webmasters using loopholes to push their sites to an undeserved high ranking. Every so often, algorithms are changed and adapted: this can have a massive effect on online businesses, as some rise and some fall in the rankings. Tips for improving your SERPs position include:

Blogging sites/software
www.blogger.com
www.movabletype.org
www.squarespace.com
www.typepad.com
www.wordpress.com (blog hosting)
www.wordpress.org (open source software download)

- **Pick a domain name that relates to your business.** Search engines match keyword searches against words in your domain name, such as www.andyherbertplumbing.com.
- **Make sure your website is easy for search engines to read.** The engines scan websites very quickly. Badly-written code can cause problems, so make sure that yours is clean and well-written. When your site is newly-built, you can register it with the major search engines to be scanned (or 'spidered', in SEO jargon). However, once your site begins to be accessed from other sites that are already in the index of each major search engine, this will begin to happen automatically. So don't worry too much about the search engines noticing updates to your site, as they will do it automatically.
- **Ensure your company name appears as text as well as a graphic.** Search engines can only 'read' words that are entered into the code as text. Images will not be read unless they have corresponding ALT tags (alternative description tags which you see when you move your mouse over them). If your company name is in your logo (a graphic), make sure it also appears on the site as ordinary text that the search engines can read.
- **Place keywords throughout your site's copy.** Internet users search the web by using keywords and key phrases. Before you start to write your content, it is useful to research the best key phrases to use. There are free and paid-for online services that can help you do this. Overture.com and Google Adwords will help you create a list of key phrases for free. Paid-for keyword selector tools, such as www.wordtracker.com are cost effective and helpful. Not only do these services provide guidance in identifying keywords, they also help you understand your market and broaden your awareness of how to attract customers. This is because they also rank the number of searches made and the effective number of competing sites, which allows you to spot gaps in the market and specific niches you may not have considered.
- **Write your copy.** Once you have selected your keywords, take two specific phrases and write a page of sales copy focused around them. For example, if you run a green consultancy that helps businesses save

❝ Ensure your company name appears as text as well as a graphic. Search engines can only 'read' words that are entered into the code as text. ❞

For articles, advice and forums on all aspects of search engine optimisation see www.seochat.com. And for discussion on search engine optimisation, web design and ecommerce, see www.sitepoint.net/forums

energy then an article on that topic could have the primary key phrase 'energy saving' and a secondary key phrase 'energy conservation'. The exact location of keyphrases in the text makes a real difference to the way search engines rank them. There are thousands of articles on the web offering specific advice about this. Given the speed with which the rules of SEO change, it is worth getting online and doing some research. A good place to start is www.sitepoint.com/forums. It can be very tempting to include too many keywords in your website copy. A few years ago, this process of 'keyword stuffing' helped improve search engine rankings. However, the major search engines have got wise to unscrupulous webmasters exploiting this weakness. To get the best balance, write your website copy with human readers in mind, but be sure to include your keywords at important points. They are particularly effective in the title bar area of your website, in headings and in the opening paragraphs.

- **Encourage other sites to link to yours.** This is the number one way of rising in the search engine rankings, especially when it comes to Google. Google operates a system called PageRank, which assesses the quality of your site for any given search based on the number of other sites (and their quality) that link to you. Each link is counted as a vote for your site, and the more votes you have the higher you will appear in the SERPs.

Jargon Buster

Search engine An online service run by companies such as Google, MSN and Yahoo! that trawls the internet to find websites that contain the word or words you have opted to look for. Most searches are completed in a few seconds.

SERPs An acronym standing for search engine results pages. This is the list of websites and webpages that your search engine displays after having completed a search for you.

SEO An acronym standing for search engine optimisation, which means trying to ensure that your website or webpage is listed close to the top of the search engine results pages (which can number into the many thousands).

Wherever possible, ask sites linking to yours to include a text link, this will help their own ranking for that phrase and yours. For example, if you are selling teapots, then a link that uses the word 'teapot' from a site that is itself about teapots is worth much more than a link that uses the text 'my son's website' from your

If your site contains interesting, useful and relevant content it will draw traffic and do at least respectably well in the search engine results page.

159

Ed runs a UK-wide business servicing lifts. He decides to launch a website to promote his business. After creating the site with the help of a web designer, he sets out to work his way up the search engine rankings. Ed knows that to earn incoming links, he needs to be seen as an authority in his niche. He therefore writes a series of articles to put on his site. Although he is not a great writer, Ed knows a lot of useful stuff about buying, installing and servicing lifts, as well as related laws on health and safety and disabled access. Very soon he has a database of thirty informative articles which also contain a good selection of important keywords. These attract a lot of attention, winning some additional business and, importantly, getting links from other sites, including lift companies who are keen to be associated with someone giving honest broker advice. Very soon Ed's order book begins to fill up as he climbs the search engine rankings.

mum's site about knitting. Link building is something of an art, and a classic example of the way the web helps people who help it. If you become a respected, popular presence in your particular corner of the internet, bringing to the web an unusual collection of products or some useful advice, you are much more likely to get the large number of links you need.

- **Operate in a niche.** We talked about the value of niche marketing in Chapter 7. Being a big fish in a small ocean is useful on the internet, too. If you are selling mobile phones, computers, or some sort of service like general programming or web design, you will be competing with hundreds of thousands of other businesses that have been around for a while and have established a good search engine ranking. If you are lucky, you might appear on the tenth page of the search results after six months of hard work. You will still get traffic, these are popular topics, after all, but you will really struggle to compete with the major players. If, however, you are offering a unique product or service, you can get on the first page very quickly. That is not to say there will not be any competition, no matter how weird or wonderful your product.

- **Include good content on your site.** One of the few rules that has survived since the very early days of internet marketing is 'content is king'. If your site contains interesting, useful and relevant content it will draw traffic and do at least respectably well in the SERPs. The best content from a search engine point of view is textual (although video sharing sites like YouTube offer a way of promoting your site using video content). Make sure all articles are well-written, linked to your home page, and contain some of your main keywords. Try to be as informative and useful as possible. By doing so you will attract incoming links from other

Case Study Priya

Priya creates designs and inscriptions for greetings cards. She has been working in the business for a while. When she first started out, in 1986, she had to rely on her contacts within the greetings card industry to win work, and most of her submissions to clients were sent by post, meaning she worked with quite long turnaround times, and often experienced delays in getting paid. Since the late 1990s, however, she has been doing more of her work on computer and sending it to her clients by email.

She would like to expand her business by working with more overseas customers. She knows the greetings card industry in the United States is huge, and there is a growing market in the Far East. She is aware, though, that because the business is design-based it is vital that her website looks as professional as possible. She hires a skilled web designer who creates a look based on some of Priya's most successful card designs. Once the site is up and running, Priya drives traffic to it using pay-per-click advertising and by participating in online industry forums.

Priya soon discovers that the internet opens up new opportunities. Within a few weeks she is getting requests for personalised and customised designs that people can print at home. Priya goes back to her web designer and asks her to adapt the website so that it has a special area for customers who are interested in personalised card design.

sites and, by default, write the kind of keyword copy that search engines like. This is another area where blogs come into their own. They are easy to update, offer a natural way of adding content to your site and tend to be popular with search engines.

- **Give it time.** Do not expect to get a high listing in the SERPs overnight. If your site contains good content relevant to your business, and you update regularly, it will rise over time. However, if despite having good content and plenty of links, your website continues to languish on page 20 or 30 of the SERPs after six months rather than beginning to climb, it might be worth seeking the advice of a reputable SEO expert.

PAY-PER-CLICK

Search engine optimisation is time-consuming, and when you are working for yourself, your time is valuable and often too short. Another way of using search engines to drive traffic to your site is to run a pay-per-click (PPC) marketing campaign.

❝ A pay-per-click campaign does not have to be time consuming or difficult and, depending on your market, it need not be particularly expensive either. **❞**

161

If you have performed a search on Google or Yahoo!, you have probably noticed that above and to the right of the main results are a number of advertisements that are relevant to your search. These are PPC ads. Businesses have registered them with the search engine, which displays them next to relevant search results. Every time a search engine user clicks an ad, the advertiser pays a fee to the search engine, hence the term 'pay-per-click'.

Starting and running a pay-per-click campaign does not have to be time consuming or difficult and, depending on your market, it need not be particularly expensive, either. There is not a set price for PPC ads. Instead, you bid a certain amount (typically stipulating an upper price that you are prepared to pay for each click). When a search is made, the search engine compares the relevant ads, and displays the ones with the highest attached bids at the top of the column of PPC ads. The more you bid, the higher your ad appears, the more clicks you get.

PPC advertising can work very well, though it is a good idea to measure the results of a campaign, and test different ads against one another. To help control costs you can place a monthly cap on your keyword expenditure. Google and Yahoo! also allow advertisers to target their advertisements at search engine users from particular geographical areas.

As well as being displayed high on the

Case Study Emma

Emma, a former recruitment consultant, has written a book that offers advice to IT specialists on how to write a good CV. She is publishing it herself, using print-on-demand technology. However, she is aware that there is a lot of competition for high positions in the SERPs. Just typing 'CV' or the American equivalent, 'resumé' into Google generates thousands of results.

So instead of simply concentrating on search engine optimisation, Emma decides to develop a buzz-marketing approach. She has already created an ecommerce website that she plans to use to sell the book direct to her customers. She adds a blog to the site, regularly updating it with hints and tips (without giving away too much of the book), as well as coverage and discussion of news stories from the IT employment sector. She seeks out similar blogs (ignoring those of her direct competitors) and begins to contribute useful and interesting comments to them. After a while, other bloggers begin to comment on her site and link to it. Her regular blogging establishes her as an authority on her subject. Before very long, three benefits have become apparent, each resulting in increased sales:

● Her search engine rank is rising steadily as other sites begin to link to her.
● Her non-search engine traffic is increasing (again, thanks to the links).

She has been approached by a number of major websites and magazines to write about her area of expertise, earning journalistic fees as well as publicity.

SERPs, PPC ads can also be displayed on private websites. Indeed, you can sign up with a number of services, including Google and Yahoo!, to carry ads on your site. This can be a great way of earning a bit of extra income, though you need to make sure that you do not end up advertising your competitors!

SOCIAL NETWORKS

Social networking sites have exploded in popularity over the last few years. A social networking site allows you to post a profile of yourself (or your business) and interact and communicate with other people and businesses.

The market leaders are www.myspace.com and www.facebook.com, which are largely aimed at the 14-25 age group. However, the idea of online networking has also taken off in the business community, with sites like www.linkedin.com and www.konnects.com offering an equivalent service to the professional and commercial sector. If you are a specialist of some sort, it is well worth looking into business networking sites. It is probably also well worth your while taking a few minutes to post profiles on MySpace and Facebook, if only because doing so allows you to post some links back to your website.

❝ Social networking sites have exploded in popularity over the last few years. A social networking site allows you to post a profile of yourself (or your business) and interact and communicate with other people and businesses. ❞

Online etiquette

Before we move on from online business, it is worth taking a quick look at some of the unwritten rules of internet etiquette.

One of the problems of online communication is that most of it is written and a lot of it (particularly blog and forum posting) takes place on the spur of the moment. If you are trying to build a buzz around your business website, it is very important that you do not accidentally annoy or upset someone. Here are some pointers to set you on the right track to a friendly, rewarding web experience:

- When you write an email, blog comment, or forum post, imagine the person you are talking to is standing right in front of you. It is easy to forget that people on the web are also real people.
- It is okay to disagree with a forum post, but take care when criticising other people. Be aware of alternative perspectives and try to make your points positively.
- Remember that irony and shades of meaning often do not come across very well in hurriedly written messages. Take care, and spell out your meaning as precisely as you can.
- Try to acknowledge emails promptly, even if it is just with a message saying 'got your email, I'll get back to you in detail in the morning'.
- When you write comments on blogs or in forums, write something useful. Simply saying hello or making a brief, useless comment as a way of drawing attention to your site is a good way of annoying people.
- It is good manners to write emails, blog comments and forum posts in grammatical English with punctuation and capital letters in the right places. Avoid using text message type abbreviations. Even worse is WRITING EVERYTHING IN CAPITAL LETTERS. This can give the same impression as shouting and most internet users consider it rude and annoying.
- Avoid spamming people. That includes sending spam email, posting on blogs and forums or promoting your business on user-editable information sites like www.wikipedia.org. Promoting yourself on social networking sites is fine, as long as you confine the promotions effort to your own profile page and do not start adding comments to other people's pages just to promote your business.

Relationships

All business has its basis in human interactions.
If you want to make a success of working for
yourself, getting along with people is crucial.
People are your customers, your employees,
your investors, your mentors.

Why relationships matter

Understanding what makes people tick is vital to building a successful business. You should develop the habit of seeing life through the eyes of your customers and your business contacts.

In a sense, this whole book is about relationships, because they form the basis of everything your business does. The success of your business is, to a very large extent, governed by the quality of the relationships you have with your:

- Existing customers.
- Potential customers.
- Past customers.
- Suppliers and subcontractors.
- Business partner(s).
- Advisers and mentors.
- Bank manager.
- Business network.
- Staff (if you have any).

We have already discussed some of these relationships in previous chapters, and we will come on to the rest shortly. Before we do, it is worth taking a look at the type of qualities that you need to be successful in any type of business relationship. Most of them are vital to all social relationships too, but it is useful to consider each one from a business point of view. These are the seven qualities of a successful relationship builder.

- **Willingness to listen.** When you are in a meeting or discussion with a client or colleague, it is important to come across as a good listener. Of course, this is vital in most types of relationship, but in business particularly so. When you are trying to sell a product or present an idea, the most important thing is to understand your customers' needs. Too many sales have been lost by an over-enthusiastic salesman who failed to pay attention to what his customer had to say. If you have ever had the impression that the person you are talking to is not really listening to you, you will know how annoying this can be. When you are having a conversation with someone, make sure they get plenty of time to ask questions and express their view.
- **Empathy.** This refers to someone's ability to identify and understand another person's situation. If you have empathy, you can see the world from somebody else's point of view. Being a good listener is key.
- **A sense of give-and-take.** You will not keep your business contacts for long if you are always asking them to scratch your back and never returning the favour. If you find yourself always

getting in touch with people to ask favours, make sure you are doing what you can to keep the score even.

- **Effort.** Time and effort invested in maintaining your business contacts will be repaid. You need to do more than just send Christmas cards to your customers and the odd bottle of wine to your contacts, you have to take a deep interest in their needs and business activities. Maintain a contacts list. Go through it periodically and make sure, as far as you can, that everyone is being 'looked after'.

❝ It is vital for your reputation and for your customers' satisfaction that you deliver your products and services when you have promised to. ❞

- **Reliability.** This is particularly important when dealing with customers, and not just in service roles. In today's marketplace, most people want instant satisfaction. Though you can never achieve the impossible, it is vital for your reputation and for your customers' satisfaction that you deliver your products and service when you have promised to. Reliability is also important when dealing with contacts, contractors and any employees you may take on. Make sure everyone is paid on time as far as your cashflow permits. A good rule of thumb is to make sure

that you put as much work into meeting your obligations as you do into pulling in your own profits.

- **Decisiveness.** You will find it hard to form lasting business relationships if you are indecisive or fail to act at important times. Decisiveness is often the key to resolving short-term problems. But your success in the future also depends on you being committed to long-term objectives, and you can only commit to them once you have made a decision. When you are faced with a project, problem or a strategic decision, form a plan and act on it. Do not keep your customers, colleagues or yourself waiting while you mess about.
- **Warmth.** This may seem obvious, but people like people who are warm and friendly. You can still be determined and demanding, but you will get so much more out of relationships if you understand the importance of investing in them. Whatever you do in life or business generally comes back to you, and a friendly, warm approach is far more likely to create the positive support you need to succeed.

Managing contacts

Even if you do not have any employees, people are still the most important part of your business, and you should approach the management of relationships with the same care as you manage the delivery of your products or service.

If your products or service require you to keep track of multiple contacts, or if they require a long lead-time, (that is, it takes you several weeks or months to go from first contact through to a sale) then a Customer Relationship Management (CRM) software package can be very useful. There are a number of applications on the market, many of them are within the price range of small businesses and some of them are free, such as. www.freecrm.com and www.sugarcrm.com.

If a CRM package is not necessary for your business, you can simply keep all your contacts' details in a spreadsheet. Not only does this provide a handy contacts list, but you can also use it to keep track of recent dealings. You can notice if a particular client goes 'quiet', and take steps to find out why this has happened. A customer list also allows you to keep track of marketing and other communications that you have sent to customers. A detailed spreadsheet of customer details and activity is an excellent tool for co-ordinating your own strategy to generate valuable repeat business.

A general contacts list is also useful, sometimes for the most unexpected reasons. If you come across a problem or an opportunity that you yourself are not fully equipped to exploit, a quick scan down a contacts list can be a big help: you can use it to identify connections between the demands of the job and the talents of your contacts.

You do not necessarily have to spend ages setting up a contacts list: most email programs (both standalone applications like Outlook and webmail systems such as Gmail and Yahoo! Mail) automatically record new contacts and allow you to organise and export your contacts list to other applications. Remember it is worth investing time in filling in as much information as you can. Knowing the name of a receptionist or a customer's husband or wife are small things that make a big difference in the way that people perceive you.

Although a lot of today's communication is by email, it is important to remember to list the details of those contacts whom you do not deal with electronically.

Customer service

Good customer service can make the difference between the success and failure of your business. It is deeply tied up with your brand, to the extent that poor levels of service can cancel out the positive effects of a good product and price.

Good customer service is one of the main drivers of repeat business, which is itself vital to the long-term success of your operation. Often, a high-quality customer experience can outweigh pricing as a competitive factor. As we will see in the case study opposite, operating as a small business can give you a huge edge over larger companies in terms of customer service, because, depending on the sector you are working in, you tend to be much closer to your customers.

Personal customer service can make a big difference. Never underestimate the importance of goodwill. Most people are not completely mercenary about where they take their business. Much of Kevin's success (see case study, right) is built on the fact that a lot of people in his town like him and want to send business his way. Of course, if his service levels dropped he could no longer rely on this. The lesson is simple: many small businesses have an advantage over larger competitors when it comes to customer service. You should exploit this advantage as much as you can.

Case Study   Kevin

Kevin is a car mechanic. He maintains a high profile around the small town where he runs his business, and is attentive to the needs of his customers. He has a van and mobile workshop, and if a customer is struggling to bring a car into his workshop, he will visit that customer's home or office and do the work there. His mobile phone is always on, and he is not the least bit bothered about taking calls on Sunday afternoons or late in the evening. Kevin is always friendly and polite with everyone and is an important member of his local community, helping out with town events, school fundraisers and his local Scout troop. Kevin enjoys doing this sort of thing for its own sake, but it is also good for his business.

There are several other garages in town, including two branches of large, national companies. Through economies of scale, they can massively undercut Kevin on price. However, Kevin's customers would rather pay extra for the superb service he offers.

❝ Operating as a small business can give you a huge edge over larger companies in terms of customer service. ❞

TECHNIQUES

Good customer service is common sense, though given the amount of bad customer service you can experience in the UK, you could be forgiven for thinking otherwise. The key thing is to remember that good customer service is built on forming a relationship with the customer. Here are some useful techniques for making sure you are treating your customers as well as you can:

- **The customer is always right.** This should go to the core of your marketing strategy. Remember that business is not about giving the market what you think it needs, but giving it what it wants. If your customers do not like your service, or cannot make your product work, you should see that as your problem, not as a failing on their part. Of course, there will always be the occasional unreasonable customer, although you will find that the types of people that are unreasonable can, oddly enough, become enthusiastic ambassadors for your business if you manage to win them over. Remember, nobody talks about average service: they talk about bad service and they talk about exceptional.

- **Bend over backwards.** Every customer is different and has slightly different needs. Large companies often use economies of scale to create one-size-fits-all solutions. As a small business your objective must be to use your size to your advantage by offering personalised customer service. Doing your best to fulfil customer requests that are that are possible but outside the usual run of what you do, is a key part of building strong, ongoing customer relationships and more likely to result in better margins and more referrals. At the same time, do not give too much away. Having a specific customer service policy (see below) will help, because it allows you to set out exactly what you are prepared to do from the start of each new customer relationship.

- **Make it part of the brand.** Good customer service should be woven into the fabric of your business to the extent that it becomes a brand value. If you employ staff, work very hard to make sure they support this aspect of your brand. Customer service training does not need to be complicated, it can be as simple as asking staff to smile and to offer help to customers. But such small actions can make an enormous difference. Nobody likes dealing with staff who seem bored, uninterested, or even worse, who look down on customers as an unwelcome hindrance. Consistently champion customer service as a key part of your brand.

> ❝ Customer service training does not need to be complicated, it can be as simple as asking staff to smile and to offer help to customers. ❞

- **Care about your customers, and let it show.** Take an interest in your customers and use technology wherever you can to help them. If you read an article online that could be of interest to a customer, send it to him, even if it is nothing to do with business. If you are passing a customer's premises two months after you have done a job for them, drop in and check that everything is OK. The likelihood is that it will be, and if it is not you have the chance to convert a negative into a positive by sorting things out. If you have a relatively small number of customers, take an interest in them. If they are business customers try to understand the needs of their businesses, after all, your success depends on theirs. If you think about your customers purely in terms of sales statistics, you will have the wrong attitude for success.
- **Be available out of hours.** This is especially important if you are providing a critical service. The rules are the same for a plumber who needs to be prepared to take calls at all hours, as they are for an international freelance worker dealing with clients in the United States. This does not mean that you need to work around the clock, or that it always has to be you that answers the telephone; you can always exploit the benefits of virtual office services. However, a client in New York will probably not want to reach your answerphone at 1pm his time because you have already finished for the day. When you are working

on an international basis, most customers understand the difficulties time zone differences can cause. But if you are regularly unavailable, they will soon start to take their business to someone who is not.
- **Follow-up.** The majority of customers who are unhappy about your product or service will probably not complain, they will just take their business elsewhere. People dislike fuss and confrontation. A good way of identifying problems is to follow-up every sale. If something has gone wrong, this is also a good way of re-establishing some of the rapport that may have been lost with a disappointed customer.

Planning point

Do not waste time sending out customer satisfaction surveys; that is passing responsibility for good service on to the customer and few will return them unless you offer an incentive.

The best way to follow-up on a sale is informally, ideally with a call followed with an email. If you follow-up your customers after they have received your product or service, you will put distance between you and the majority of your competitors. If you then identify and sort out a problem, you will be remembered for the quality of your service and not for the problem. If you can also leave your customers with a special offer or discount on their next purchase, you have already laid the groundwork for your next sale.

- **Return calls and emails quickly.** We talked about the importance of etiquette in the online environment in Chapter 8. You should be aware that being prompt when replying to customer enquiries is not just a case of offering good service, it makes good business sense, too. If a potential customer has approached you with a sales enquiry there is a good chance he or she has approached one of your competitors. Respond quickly and you have a greater chance of winning the customer.

- **Invoice promptly.** If you are dealing with business customers it is important to submit your invoice on time. This may seem a ridiculous point to make, but in reality, the writing and sending of invoices is one of those awkward little jobs that is easy to put off when other matters are pressing. Prompt invoicing allows your customers to plan and manage their cashflow more easily. That is not to say they will pay you promptly, but sending the invoice in means it will also be off your 'to do' list and on their system.

- **Say 'sorry' when you get it wrong.** Everybody, and every business, makes mistakes. When you get something wrong, remember the customer's perspective. They can get upset and sometimes angry. This is your opportunity to put it right. You do not want a disappointed customer spreading the news that your business is no good. Fixing the problem, at your expense, can make all the difference. Remember to say 'sorry'. It is pointless fixing something begrudgingly, so give them something extra. This is a common tactic in restaurants: a free desert or bottle of wine may mean reduced profit in the short term, but it can help save a customer you might otherwise have lost.

You will notice that we have not mentioned anything about pricing. The price you put on your products and services is completely unrelated to customer service. You should not see a low price or special offer in terms of 'doing the customer a favour' and an excuse for a poor level of care. That is not to say there are not niche markets for no-frills services. In the air travel industry, for example, many customers are more than happy to give up their on-board meal and land thirty miles from their destination in exchange for a better deal. Just do not confuse no-frills service with no service at all. Customers tend to judge price and service levels independently of one another. If you slash your prices, but offer poor customer service, you could still find yourself being

> **❝ Being prompt when replying to customer enquiries is not just a case of offering good service, it makes good business sense, too. ❞**

beaten by a more expensive competitor who simply puts a bit more effort into maintaining good customer relationships.

Although part of the beauty of running a small business is that you can tailor the required level of service to the individual customer, it is a good idea to have set customer service policies which you make a point of sticking to. This avoids the type of problem that comes up when you offer a particularly high level of service to a customer, word gets around and suddenly everyone wants to be treated that way.

Your customer service policy can still be generous, but writing it down and making it public sets acceptable boundaries that can not only save you time and money but, just as important, create a major selling point. If you have developed a computer program, a year's free telephone support is worth a lot to your customers. But, plan carefully and make sure you are not giving away too much, or making promises that you cannot deliver.

Planning point

Try to develop policies on:

- delivery times
- refunds
- level of after-sales support
- discounting

Networking

Building networks of business partners and contacts is a vital skill. As your business grows you will find that, with a bit of effort, your network grows too.

When you are an employee, your networks tend to be your work colleagues, business contacts, friends and associates. These networks are useful but they do not necessarily put money in your bank. When you work for yourself, your network takes on a different role. Each of your contacts becomes a potential customer, referrer, partner, and joint venture opportunity.

When you set-up your own business, one of the biggest problems that you often need to overcome is spreading the news. You will not develop your business if you keep it a secret and yet many businesses fail to promote themselves. "Oh I didn't know Alan did that!" is an expression that is all too often heard when Alan has actually been in business for ten years. There is nothing to be embarrassed about being in business. It is something to be proud of. You have taken the decision, you have gone and done it, and now you need to make sure that everybody knows about it.

Your network should initially consist of all the people you know well enough to talk to about your business, call upon for help, or who might ask you for assistance themselves. You need to build on that foundation. Be interested in people.

You will be amazed what happens when you start talking to others about what they do, what you do and what you have in common.

> ❝ You will be amazed what happens when you start talking to others about what they do, what you do and what you have in common. ❞

It is very often said that success is a not a question of what you know, but who you know. That is certainly the case when it comes to starting-up. Whenever you do jobs that customers are happy with, remember to ask them if they know anyone else who might be interested in your product or service. If they volunteer some contacts, thank them and follow-up the information without delay. If business comes to you in this way, make a point of going back to your original customer and offering thanks. Buy your referrer a small gift, you can be sure that word of your kindness will soon get out.

Planning point

An important benefit of having a large network is that you can refer people to other businesses. After a while, people will come to you in the knowledge that you are likely to know someone who can help them. Once you are in that position, it becomes much easier to build your business. By making referrals you increase the chances of getting referred customers back as repeat customers for your own business. Some networking clubs operate on this basis.

Many people who have been in business for a while often say, 'I never advertise' and that is often the case. They do not need to because they have a constant stream of referrals.

Fortunately, because everyone in business recognises the value of networking, there are hundreds organisations dedicated to building links between different members of the business community.

- Local areas often have dedicated chambers of commerce. These are organisations that offer contacts, social events and a background for co-operation between businesses in a local area. They are excellent sources of advice, and often a good place to pick up some informal mentoring if you are new to business. Chambers have also become involved in representing business in local and political forums. They are funded on a subscription basis, and annual fees are usually in the region of a few hundred pounds. This, however, can be money very well spent.

- Further afield, you may find that there are national (and international) trade federations representing businesses in your sector and related trades. Internet specialists, for example, can join the UK Web Design Association (www.ukwda.org) while builders can apply for membership of the Federation of Master Builders (www.fmb.org.uk). Some trade unions offer support to self-employed workers. For example, professional musicians can benefit from membership of the Musicians' Union (www.musiciansunion.org.uk), while qualified, freelance tutors can join teaching unions such as the Association of Teachers and Lecturers (ATL) and the National Union of Teachers (NUT). Membership of a Union or federation often offers networking benefits as well as legal protection and insurance.

- Business clubs are similar to chambers of commerce, but are less formal and tend to focus solely on the networking side of things. The cost of joining (and the quality of what scheduled events the clubs offer) varies, so it is a good idea to do some research. Clubs are often worth joining just for the social side: few self-employed people enjoy the perks and 'jollies' on offer to many corporate workers. Business Clubs often organise discounted days out to sporting, cultural and activity-based events to make up for this.

- Networking events, business breakfasts and referral clubs have grown in popularity over the past few years. Often organised by business clubs, chambers of commerce and private networking companies, they offer business people working in related sectors the opportunity to get together and build relationships and refer business. You can usually find networking events in your local area. Specialist sectors are also often organised on a national basis. They tend to be rather intense, with everyone trying to get to know everyone else in a short period of time, but that is all part of the fun. Major cross-sector networking events are organised by national and global businesses such as First Tuesday (www.firsttuesday.com) and The Glasshouse (www.theglasshouse.net). You are likely to find major networking events useful if you're planning to build a rapidly-growing business within a flourishing, in-demand sector. Corporate events such as these cost money, but for certain types of business they are invaluable. Do not forget to take plenty of business cards!

- Another great place to wield that business card is at trade shows and exhibitions. Organised by a variety of private and public organisations, these are valuable events for meeting new people across a wide range of industries. Unless you see a real opportunity to sell your products or services, you do not always need to book a stall or benefit from a trade show. Wandering around exhibitions and talking to exhibitors and other attendees is a great way to build your network.

Online networking

Finally, don't neglect the networking possibilities the internet offers. We talked about online social networks in Chapter 8. There are also a number of useful online business clubs and forums, for example www.businessclub365.com, www.ukbusinessforums.co.uk and www.startupsuk.co.uk, all of which offer networking opportunities as well as a variety of special offers to members.

 To find your local chamber of commerce, see the British Chambers of Commerce website, www.chamberonline.co.uk

Day-to-day running

Starting your business and getting your first sale are major milestones and you should congratulate yourself on passing them. But the real work has only just begun. It is what you do on a day-to-day basis that will ultimately deliver long-term success. This chapter will help you achieve that.

Managing your time

You will quickly discover that there is a lot of truth in the old saying 'time is money'. The quality of day-to-day results depends on how you use your most critical resource; your time.

One of the major differences between self-employment and working for someone else is that the money you earn is directly linked to your productivity. In a salaried job it is possible to coast and still look busy and, if you manage a team, ride on the back of others' success.

When you run your own business you have to deal with the brutal truth that if you do not deliver, you do not get paid. Because the amount of work you can do is governed by the amount of time you have available to you, you have to think very carefully about how to use that time effectively. Simply working hard is not enough; you have to 'work smart'. Think of your role in terms of four key areas of responsibility:

- **Delivery and operations.** This is what you need to do to get paid. It is pointless spending time on the preparation if, when you go to market, you do not actually sell anything. You have not got a business until somebody buys what you are offering.
- **Administration.** This is the area where many entrepreneurs and trades people struggle. They can do the business, but fail to do the paperwork. They know they are busy because they are working ten hours a day, but do not know how much they are making because they never stop to work it out. Even worse, because they are too busy they often do not invoice until the bank bounces their cheques, or there is no food on the table.
- **The future.** It is very easy to get bogged down in the daily running of your business. You know the work is coming in because you are busy and organised. The problem is you are giving no thought to the future. If you do not have ideas about what you want to be doing in five or ten years' time, the chances are you will still be doing exactly what you are doing right now.
- **Marketing.** You are busy today and next week, but what happens in a month's time? What is going to happen when things quieten down at Christmas or in the middle of the summer? We have been stressing the importance

❝ The amount of work you can do is governed by the amount of time you have available to you, so think carefully about how to use your time effectively. ❞

of effective marketing throughout the book. As well as being part of your long-term strategy, it should also be a central part of the day-to-day running of your business. Day-to-day marketing is the work you do now to bring in business tomorrow, next month or next year, it should be a constant activity. If you are working for a client, leave him with a brochure, business cards and a list of other services. If you are a landscape gardener, do not work anywhere without leaving your 'A' board outside. If you are a beautician give each client a list of the other treatments that you also offer.

TIPS AND TRICKS

There are lots of things you can do to manage your time. Ultimately, you have to do what is effective for you and what suits your business. Here are some tried-and-tested techniques to get your started:

- **List and prioritise your tasks.** A task list does not only give your day structure, ticking off the jobs one-by-one can also be an incentive in itself. As you become more experienced, you will learn that different jobs are often best done at different times of the day, so you might want to think about allocating yourself a regular timetable. The extent to which you are able to do this will be governed by your working environment and the needs of your customers. For example, it is easier for a freelance writer to work in the middle of the night than a tree surgeon. A good trick is to make the writing of your job list the last task of the day.

If you put together a timetable the evening before, you can hit the ground running as soon as you start work. One word of advice: do not be too ambitious in terms of what you can achieve in a day. It is very easy to get demoralised when you are only halfway through the list of jobs you have promised yourself you will get done. Work hard, but be realistic.

- **Work efficiently.** If you are well-organised you will waste far less time looking for things, so invest some time in organising your work space. Working efficiently also means being able to focus on your job for a prolonged period of time. If you are doing something that involves a lot of hard concentration, you might find that you squeeze more productive time out of your day if you take regular breaks. You could follow the advice given to students revising for exams: 50 minutes on, 10 minutes off

---

How to manage your daily postbag

- If it is irrelevant, throw it away immediately.
- If it is a bill, put in the 'Bills To Be Paid' file which you go through on a weekly basis.
- If it is a customer enquiry, put it in the 'Customer Enquiries' file which you go through daily.
- If it is a product, service or an article that you are interested in, put it in the 'To Read' file, which you pick up when you want to take a break.
- If it is a bank statement, file immediately and make a monthly check that your incoming cash, outgoing costs and current balance add up. (This process is known as 'reconciling' your account.)

Golden rules for filing documents on your computer

- Save all your documents in the Documents folder. Do not use your desktop as a dumping ground, or develop the 'I'll file it later' mentality. Remember the 'Do it now' rule.
- Create folders and sub folders within Documents. Identify a clear structure and stick to it. Create folders for Sales, Marketing, Ideas, Finance, Plans, Personal, Administration, Operations, Customers and whatever else you need for your particular business. Within each folder create sub-folders. So, for example, within Finance you may have Management Accounts, Bank and Investors (if you have any). Using logical structures like this saves hours in the long term.
- Set up your email application to manage incoming messages from different sources. It is useful, for example, to have messages from a sales enquiry address on your website delivered to a different folder from the one personal messages are sent to. If you are working with other people on a project, you can set-up your email program to deliver all mail from their addresses to a project-specific folder.

a rule that you take action on every piece of mail you open every day.

- **Manage your virtual space.** Computers are wonderful things. Documents always stay where you put them, and there is a useful search function to find any file you need in seconds. However, if you find that you are using the search facility too often, you need a better system for filing.
- **Avoid distractions.** This is a particular danger for people working from home. It can be too easy to start doing the crossword, watching daytime TV or randomly surfing the internet when you are supposed to be working. When deadlines start pressing, you end up working round the clock to finish a job that you could have completed comfortably had you been more organised. When you work for yourself you need to be disciplined, that means shutting out distractions and focusing on your goals.
- **Know yourself.** You will probably find you are more efficient at some times of the day than at others. Most people, though by no means all, are at their brightest during the morning and early-to-mid evening, slowing down after lunch and late at night. Try to plan your day's work around these natural cycles: if you fit the typical model you will find heavy analytical or creative work is easier in the morning and hard going in the afternoon (think back to your school days – remember those after-lunch maths lessons?). Fill up less productive hours of the day with more mundane tasks, or if you

for three to four hours followed by a half-hour break. When you are working, work hard. The same principle, obviously, goes for manual work. Your health, fitness and ability to concentrate are crucial, so do not work until you drop. You will be more efficient if you plan regular breaks into your time.

- **Do it now.** You can save so much time by taking action as soon as it can be taken, rather than putting off jobs until tomorrow. For example, have can, knock off and do something for else for a few hours before returning to your work in the evening.

❝ A saving in time is usually a saving in money in the long run. ❞

- **Motivate yourself.** Some jobs bring their own motivation because they are interesting or because they result in fast profits. Others, like keeping your accounts, or completing VAT and tax returns, are much less engaging and all too easy to postpone. Give yourself rewards for completing dull tasks, even if it is just an extra biscuit with your cup of tea. Tiny incentives can be motivating.
- **Farm out.** Do you really need to do the mundane jobs that don't require your high-level skills? Why spend hours stuffing envelopes when you could get it done by someone else? If you have children, this can be a great way for them to earn some extra pocket money. Try to identify those jobs that do not really need your abilities and skills and look for ways to get someone else to do them. You will have to pay, of course, but a saving in time is usually a saving in money in the long run.

Above all, you need to be self-disciplined. If you find this difficult, do not despair, it does not necessarily mean you are not

Jargon Buster

Documents folder The folder on your computer where word-processing and spreadsheet documents are usually stored. Known as 'My Documents' in earlier versions of Windows, it is labelled 'Documents' in Windows Vista and all versions of Mac OS.

cut out to work for yourself. You just need to be aware of your strengths and weaknesses, working to the former and trying to reduce the effects of the latter.

Working for yourself lets you create a working style that suits you best. When you are in paid employment, working styles are more or less thrust upon you. Not everybody is perfectly suited to the office-type of working style that involves steadily progressing through your daily tasks. Workers in creative roles, for example, often work in quite short, intensive bursts punctuated by periods of apparently not doing very much while they reflect on what they have done or what is coming up next. The trick is to find the style that suits you, your chosen business model, and crucially, your target market.

Administration and accounting

Not many people like looking after administrative work, but it has to be done. Luckily, technology has made things easier. If you get a good system set up it will minimise the time you need to keep administration up to date.

A lot of business advice and guidance focuses on filling in tax returns, sorting out your accounts and other fairly dull tasks. It is easy to get the impression that running a business mostly consists of sitting behind a desk doing a mountain of paperwork. It is certainly true that if you choose to expand your business and take on staff, the amount of administration that is required of you will increase. However, by that stage you could well be in a position to hire someone to do most of it for you. If you are self-employed with no employees, you should find that administration and accounting takes up a minimal amount of time.

&& If you do not feel confident about managing your books, you can hire a bookkeeper for a few hours a month.))

ACCOUNTING

Accounting is not difficult. Most of it revolves about sorting out receipts, invoicing on time, keeping your business and personal finances separate, and tracking all of this in a timely and organised manner. If you do not feel confident about managing your books, you can hire a bookkeeper for a few hours a month. Alternatively, a friend or family member may be more than happy to help out.

When you start out in business it can be very useful to take one of the short courses that HM Revenue and Customs runs for start-ups. These cover aspects of accounting and tax, and generally give you pointers on how to prepare accounts in a way that HMRC likes. Remember that if your business turns over less than £15,000 in any given year, you do not even need to submit detailed accounts with your tax return. More or less everything

 The formulas for working out the amount of tax you can offset against various benefits in kind change with reasonable regularity. A tax accountant can advise you, or you can find all the information you need on the HMRC website, see www.hmrc.gov.uk

How to avoid common problems associated with preparing accounts

- **Missing or incomplete records.** Create the habit of organising and recording your expense receipts frequently. It is a good idea to do this at least once a month. If you have a business credit or debit card, use it for as much as you can, as it will make everything much easier to account for. If it is a credit card, remember to clear the balance at every payment date to save you paying unnecessary interest charges. You should keep receipts for all your business expenses, and if you use your car for business, detailed records of your business mileage, too. If receipts go missing you can still include the expense in your accounts, but if you get investigated by HMRC, more than one or two missing receipts could cause you a problem.

- **Foreign currency payments.** Make sure you work out the exchange rate when you receive the payment, not six months later when you are sitting down to prepare the accounts. If the exchange rate has fallen in the meantime you could wind up paying more tax than you have to. If it has risen and HMRC work out what you have done, they will be after you for the extra money they think you owe them. Do not neglect the built-in accounting features that many online payment systems have. PayPal, for example, keeps detailed records of all your transactions and (in the case of foreign currency payments) tracks the exchange rate at the date of payment. These records can be exported into a spreadsheet and integrated into your main account.

- **Delayed accounting.** There are real benefits to doing your accounts as you go and reviewing your business on a monthly basis. This gives you an up-to-date picture of your performance and the chance to amend your business model if profitability or sales are down. You can also test any changes, including new marketing strategies and product offers. You are also far more likely to account properly for all your expenses and, as a result, pay less tax.

- **Calculating expenses.** When it comes to calculating your expenses, most day-to-day business costs can be fully offset against tax. Other expenses like running your car, utility costs and the cost of IT equipment can be offset subject to rules provided by the HMRC. For example, there are different ways you can calculate tax-deductible expenses related to your car. You can either claim for your total expenses less a proportion for personal use, or, alternatively, you can claim a flat rate of 40p per mile for the first 10,000 miles and 25p a mile thereafter.

you need to know about filling in a tax return can be found on the HMRC website, www.hmrc.gov.uk, or by picking up the necessary leaflets at your local tax office.

If you choose to operate as a limited company, your administrative duties are slightly increased by the legal requirement to submit yearly accounts to Companies House, though again, this does not need to be hard work. If you register for VAT the burden also increases, as it does if you take on employees.

The professionals

A good accountant can be a tremendous asset to your business. However, you will save yourself money in accounting fees if you pay him just to do your accounting, and not your administration as well. If you roll up once a year at your accountant's office with a sheaf of bank statements, invoices and a shoebox full of expense receipts, he or she will sort them out for you, but you will be charged handsomely for the time it takes to do that.

Accountants are worth their fees because they are familiar with all the latest tax regulations and the best ways to use those regulations to pay as little tax as legally possible. If you are running a very small business with no employees, your accountant will cost maybe £300 or £400 a year in fees. If your business starts to expand, a good accountant will look after your tax, manage your payroll, and depending on your status, oversee your VAT returns, create your statutory returns and forward them to Companies House.

One step down the professional ladder, you will find bookkeepers. These tend to be freelancers with accounting experience who will compile your accounts for you on a weekly or monthly basis, saving you the time and trouble. Their fees are lower than qualified accountants and many are supported by qualifications recognised by the Institute of Bookkeepers.

Jargon Buster

Companies House The London-based government organisation that registers, monitors and keeps records of all UK companies. All limited companies must be registered with Companies House, sole traders do not have to.

Creditors The people and businesses that your business owes money.

Debtors The people and businesses that owe your business money.

Margin The profit you make on a product or service, considered as the proportion of the selling price that isn't eaten up by expenses.

Managing cashflow

It is often said that more businesses fail because of cashflow problems than because of a lack of profits. In the early stages of your business, careful cashflow management is vital – but even when you are established, it is a task that never really goes away.

Ultimately, your business has to generate its own cash in the form of profit. But payments do not always come your way when you need them, and it is important to look at other ways of getting your hands on cash when you need to settle your bills. If you run into cashflow problems to the extent that you cannot meet your liabilities, you can run into severe problems. This may not always be down to your own mismanagement, frequently it can be caused by actions of others. For example, if one of your major customers goes bankrupt and fails to settle a large debt, this could have a damaging effect on your business.

You need to seriously consider the structure of your business, particularly if you are exposed to large transactions with account customers. If you are a sole trader and become unable to pay your bills, your creditors (the people and businesses you owe money to) can have you declared insolvent (bankrupt). As a sole trader you are personally liable for the whole of your debt, so if the worst comes to the worst you are at the mercy of the Official Receiver, who can dispose of your property, including your house, to settle your debt. These days, efforts are usually made to set up Individual Voluntary Arrangements (IVAs) before declaring individuals insolvent. An IVA is a plan agreed with creditors to pay off debt in manageable instalments. Even so, in this situation the risk of insolvency is very real, and something you need to think about seriously if you are setting up as a sole trader.

66 If you are considering offering credit terms, you can do it through a third party rather than financing it yourself. 99

If you are running a limited company or a limited liability partnership, all the assets of the business can be sold to meet your debt. The whole point of limited liability is that you are not personally responsible for your company's debt, because in a legal sense the business is responsible for its own debts. You are only liable up to the amount of initial capital you put into the business. Remember, though, that most lenders require personal guarantees for company loans, so if your company goes to the wall your bank may still be able to sell your assets to meet your liability. Additionally, if it can be proved in court that you were deliberately negligent or did not run the company in a proper fashion, you can be declared liable for the company's debts. Such circumstances can also result in your being banned from holding company directorships for a period of time, usually several years.

So it is a pretty good idea to keep the cash coming in and your creditors paid! Mostly, that means keeping close to your customers, being aware of their creditworthiness and making sure they pay you on time.

Some cashflow problems are worse than others. If, for example, you are selling items direct to the public, you should get paid at the point of sale. If you are considering offering credit terms, you can do it through a third party rather

Methods for financing cashflow

- **Credit cards and overdrafts.** We have already talked about how useful these can be for start-up and initial running costs, (see Chapter 6). They can also be useful with cashflow management in the early days of running your business. Decent credit arrangements will allow you to settle debts quickly and build-up a good relationship with your suppliers. However, be careful not to let too much debt build up on your cards and overdraft. At times when there is a decent amount of cash available in your business, make reducing your debts a priority, it will save you a lot on interest payments and will free up spare credit for the next time you need it.
- **Factoring.** If you regularly struggle to bring in payments on time and this is having an adverse effect on your cashflow, you might consider using a factor. A debt factoring company will pay you the amount outstanding, less a fee, as soon as you issue an invoice. It will then pursue the debt itself. This can be a very good way of getting paid quickly, even if you do not get the full amount. On the other hand, it can affect your relationship with your customers, particularly smaller businesses who tend to dislike being pursued by efficient debt collectors at an early stage in the payment cycle. It can also, rightly or wrongly, indicate to others that you are experiencing financial problems. Depending on your industry, this could adversely affect your brand and reputation.
- **Supplier credit.** If you have a regular supplier, you can ask for an account whereby goods are provided to you on credit. This is useful, as you can sell things before you pay for them or their component materials, keeping your business cash-positive. Suppliers allocate credit in accordance with their assessment of each customer's ability to pay. In general, you start off by paying cash for the first few orders from a supplier, and once you have build up a reputation, a credit arrangement can be introduced. By consistently paying promptly you can gradually increase your credit limit.

than financing it yourself. This may reduce your profit margins (the credit supplier will charge you a fee) but it ensures that you get paid in time to settle your own debts.

Case Study   Angie

Angie is a corporate caterer, providing a food and drink service to companies and public sector organisations running social or promotional events. Managing cashflow can be difficult for her. She has many cash expenses, including staff, transport and food buying costs. Her difficulty is that her clients are often slow to pay her, invoices get stuck for days on the desks of council officers and accounts staff, leaving her business with very little cash. This is a risky position to be in. Angie knows that her clients are almost certain to pay eventually, as they are public bodies or established businesses. However, she sometimes needs to make use of extended credit facilities, especially when a group of invoices are late being paid. Fortunately, Angie has a good relationship with her bank manager, who understands the nature of her business and is more than happy to provide the upfront cash she needs, knowing that Angie will be paid eventually.

Bad debts are difficult things to handle. If one of your customers becomes insolvent, it can take a long while to get the money you are owed. If the debtor's total liquidated assets do not add up to the total amount of debt, a priority payment system kicks in. This means that HM Revenue and Customs takes what it is owed before business creditors can be paid. In these situations, you are unlikely to get the whole debt repaid, and if you do, it may be a long time coming.

Cashflow forecasts (see page 80) are a must have element of any business plan. Once you are established they will continue to play an important role, particularly when you are going through periods of expansion, major expenditure or a difficult patch. Creating a cashflow forecast is simple. Using a spreadsheet program like Excel you make a list of the payments coming into your business against the payments going out. For example a business with yearly costs of £50,000 and an income of £85,000, works out as a profit of £35,000. However, there are periods during the year when finances are under pressure because costs are being made before payments are received. You would typically use a cashflow forecast in conjunction with a Profit and Loss forecast (see page 82) to negotiate an overdraft facility with your bank to alleviate problems like this.

For more information on debt factoring, see Which? Essential Guides *Managing Your Debt* or to find a member of the Factors and Discount Association (FDA), see www.thefda.org.uk

STATE BENEFITS

One of the best ways to keep your cash flowing smoothly is to take as little of it as possible out of the business to pay yourself. That is easier said than done, of course, for you still have to eat and pay the mortgage.

However, you may be able to reduce the amount you draw from your business by taking advantage of state benefits. These can be particularly useful if you are not making very much money, or if you have to reduce your workload due to pregnancy or illness.

Working Tax Credit

The Working Tax Credit system is designed to help people on low incomes by reducing the amount of tax they pay. It can be particularly useful for keeping your personal finances on track if you are just starting in business and your profits are low. As well as straightforward credit against your tax bill, the system can include some childcare support, and extra benefits are also payable to a number of categories of claimant, including people with disabilities

and people over the age of 50 who have recently come back to work after spending a period on benefit.

Nine out of ten families with children are eligible for tax credit. But that doesn't mean that you have to have children in order to qualify.

Maternity Allowance

Depending to a large degree on who looks after your offspring, having children will inevitably affect your productivity and income. Most companies and organisations support employed parents with a raft of benefits and perks including: paid and unpaid maternity leave, paid and unpaid paternity leave, and 'parenting days' (where you might need a day off to care for a sick child or to look after a child who has a day closure from school).

All too often, when you are self-employed, however, you will be living in a situation where if you do not work, you do not earn. To help alleviate this situation (albeit only partly) for self-employed parents and prospective parents, the government does provide some benefits, although sadly, not paternity allowance. The main benefit aimed at self-employed mothers is Maternity Allowance. However, you may also be eligible to receive extra financial support through Child Benefit, Tax Credits and the Sure Start Maternity Grant.

❝ Depending to a large degree on who looks after your offspring, having children will inevitably affect your productivity and income. ❞

HMRC has a simple online calculator, which will give you an immediate indication of your eligibility for tax credits, see www.taxcredits.inlandrevenue.gov.uk/Qualify/DIQHousehold.aspx

From 1 April, 2007, Maternity Allowance pays a standard weekly rate of £112.75 or 90 per cent of your average weekly earnings (before tax), whichever is the smaller, for a maximum of 39 weeks. You may also work for ten days within those 39 weeks. To claim Maternity Allowance, you need to complete the form MA1, (available from your local Jobcentre Plus or as a download from the website www.direct.gov.uk). You can claim as soon as you have been pregnant for 26 weeks, although you will also need to submit evidence of when your baby is due. You can do this through the completion of a maternity certificate, MATB1, which should be given to you by your doctor or midwife.

To be eligible for Maternity Allowance, you need to be registered as self-employed and paying Class 2 National Insurance Contributions. You also need to have been at work for at least 26 of the 66 weeks before your baby is due and have earned a minimum average of £30 for half of those 26 weeks.

Incapacity Benefit

If you become ill or are injured and are unable to work, you may be able to claim Incapacity Benefit (IB). IB is a state benefit paid out to self-employed people who are too ill to work and have been paying National Insurance Contributions. Eligibility is also dependent on where you have been living or working, your age and how long you have been unable to work through ill health.

If you are eligible to claim, you will be paid one of three different weekly rates.

The lower short-term rate is £61.35 and the higher is £72.55. The long-term basic rate is £81.35.

You can claim Incapacity Benefit online via www.direct.gov.uk or through contacting your local Jobcentre Plus office.

Business software

If you are starting a business you probably already have a computer. But are you making the most of it? Too many business users do not get the value they could from their IT because they do not realise the power it really has.

In this section we are going to take an overview of business-related software as it stands in 2007. The software sector changes quickly, even by the standards of the internet. Exciting new business software appears all the time. It is a good idea to keep an eye on the market so you can spot the packages that could make a difference to your business.

OFFICE SOFTWARE

Office software has developed hugely over the past decade. The current market leader is Microsoft Office.

Different versions of Office also include Publisher (for desktop publishing), OneNote (note taking), Visio (diagramming software) and various other applications.

Microsoft Office is not the only office package on the market, though it is considered the industry standard and runs on both PC and Mac platforms. Alternatives include Apple's AppleWorks suite and OpenOffice. The latter is free, open source software. Using OpenOffice is a great way of saving money, particularly if business software is not a core component of your business. It can create

---

Microsoft Office: core applications

- **Word.** A comprehensive word processing program that allows you to create everything from a one-page letter to a detailed, illustrated book-length document. It also has functionality for creating web pages.
- **Excel.** A spreadsheet program that allows you to manipulate figures and perform calculations on large sets of data. Excel is a vital small business accounting too, and is also useful for

keeping track of orders and stock, as well as making cashflow and profit-and-loss forecasts.
- **PowerPoint.** A program that allows you to create detailed audio-visual displays. PowerPoint is an essential tool for making presentations to clients, investors and lenders.
- **Outlook.** A comprehensive email and personal organisation program.

and save files that are fully compatible with Microsoft applications. You can download it from www.openoffice.org.

OpenOffice is a less satisfactory solution if you are going to be doing a lot of IT-based work, as it is not compatible with some features of Microsoft Office. If, for example, you are exchanging a lot of documents with clients you may wish to use Microsoft's 'track changes' feature which allows you to record and comment on all changes made to a document through its various revisions. The tracking abilities of OpenOffice are rather more limited, and are not yet fully compatible with MS Office.

Project management

If you are working on a project with a number of individuals or businesses it can be very useful to use project management software, which simplifies the task of managing resources and personnel and keeps track of what it going on at any particular time over the course of a project.

Microsoft Project, which comes with some versions of Office, is a very useful project management tool. Also worth investigating is Basecamp (www.basecamphq.com), a web-based application available by subscription, allowing document sharing and project management. If you want a completely free project management and sharing service, try Google Docs (www.docs.google.com), which offers free, online, browser-based word-processing and spreadsheet software that can be shared among multiple users.

If you are working on a project with a number of individuals or businesses it can be very useful to use project management software.

Tax and accounting

You do not have to rely on Excel or other spreadsheet applications to do all your calculations for you. There are a number of useful pieces of software that are specially designed to help you sort out your accounts. They especially come in useful as your business becomes more complex.

The major suppliers of accounting software for small businesses in the UK are Sage and Intuit. Useful small business-focused software also includes Kashflow (www.kashflow.co.uk), TurboCash (www.turbocashuk.com a free, open source product) and TaxCalc (www.taxcalc.com). The latter is particularly useful as it is designed with the UK self-assessment market in mind, and integrates smoothly with the HMRC online system for filing self-assessed tax returns.

Jargon Buster

Open source software Mainly free software programs with licenses that allow users to run them for any purpose. They are also open to modification or development, and allow users to redistribute copies of either the original or modified program without having to pay royalties to previous developers.

GOVERNMENT DEPARTMENT SHAKE-UP

The government departments with responsibilities for business and innovation underwent a massive re-organisation within the first few days of Prime Minister Gordon Brown's premiership.

On becoming Prime Minister in June 2007, one of the first things Gordon Brown did was to abolish the Department of Trade and Industry (DTI). For many years, the DTI had operated as the government's main Department with a responsibility towards business and commerce.

In its place, a new ministry has been created, the Department for Business, Enterprise and Regulatory Reform (DBERR). However, DBERR's remit isn't exactly the same as that of the old DTI. It has also taken over responsibility for the Better Regulation Executive from the Cabinet Office. Many veteran business owners claim that the amount of regulation and red tape they have had to cope with has increased massively over the past ten years. DBERR's aim is to streamline and simplify UK business regulation. One of the most useful features of the government's current approach to regulatory reform, is that it actively encourages suggestions and ideas from the business sector. Take a look at the Better Regulation website (www.betterregulation.gov.uk) to find out more.

DBERR retains responsibility for Business Link, although international trade is now a joint concern, shared between DBERR, the Department for International Development and the Foreign and Commonwealth Office. However, assistance with international trading for small businesses, and incentive schemes such as Passport to Export, will continue to be accessible via Business Link and its UK Trade and Investment Enquiry Line (020 7215 8000).

The former DTI's department for small businesses (the Small Business Service) also continues as before under DBERR. Information on the services available can be accessed from the DBERR main website, www.dberr.gov.uk or from www.sbs.gov.uk.

DBERR is responsible for supporting the new Business Council for Britain, which aims to foster ties between business and government. The Council includes senior representatives of UK-based businesses among its membership. For issues it feels are particularly important, the Council has the power to establish Special Commissions to make recommendations for reform.

Another new department created by Gordon Brown in June 2007 is the Department for Innovation, Universities and Skills (DIUS). DIUS has been given responsibilities previously held by the DTI for science and innovation, along with a remit for further and higher education, training and skills that were previously part of the Department for Education and Skills. The Department has been charged with a long-term vision to ensure that Britain has the skilled workforce it needs in order to compete successfully in a global economy.

The long term

If your business takes off you could be running it for the rest of your working life. That's no small commitment: we've already seen how self-employment can affect your life. In this final chapter it is time to look at how it could affect your future.

Planning for the future

When you are tied up in the day-to-day running of a business, it can become very difficult to focus on the long term. However, it is important to look after your own needs as well as those of your business, and that means planning for the future.

If you move on from employment and successfully establish your own business, it is a reasonable bet, that for the first time in your life, you have your future in your own hands. What is that future going to look like? What are you going to be doing in five years? How hard are you going to be working? How much time will you be spending with your family? Where are you going to be living? Where is your business going to be? What is your business going to look like? What changes will you need to make all this happen?

You would be surprised how many self-employed people give little thought to these questions. When you are running a business it is all too easy to live life from one day to the next, with planning reserved strictly for working matters.

> **❝ It is worth taking time to think about the long term, and where you want your business to take you. ❞**

But you have to live and, presumably, one of the reasons you have chosen to work for yourself is that you want to live in a particular way. As well as thinking about the good of your business, you have to think about your own long-term welfare. It is as vital to your business as it is to you and your family, and unless your operation has expanded very dramatically, you will almost certainly remain your business's key asset.

LIFE CHANGES

It is worth taking time to think about the long term, and where you want your business to take you. You do not necessarily have to think too hard about this while you are going through the hectic process of starting up, but it is important at some stage to consider your long-term life goals. What do you want to achieve?

Maybe you just want to get rich. Fair enough, but many a successful entrepreneur will tell you that one certain route to failure is to go into business with the sole objective of making lots of money. The key is to get the business, the market, and the products and services right. If you do that there is a very good chance that money will follow. But let us assume your ambitions are based on a bit more than a simple desire to make a fortune.

What exactly do you want your business to bring you?

You may wish to retire early, or make enough money to travel the world, build up a nest egg, pay off your mortgage, work at home so you can watch your children grow up, or create a business empire that you can pass on to your children one day.

Time for some more questions. How long do you want to work? If your work is physical, do you want to be making the same exertions in five or ten years' time? What about your business's value, will you need to sell it to realise your ambitions? How much is it going to be worth? Say something happened outside of your control, you became ill for example, and you were unable to continue, what would happen? For all of these reasons, it is worthwhile thinking about an exit strategy, even at the earliest stage of starting-up. Investors always consider an exit plan and they are only investing money, you are investing your whole life.

So let us imagine the clocks have moved forward and, for whatever reason, you are calling it a day. What will your options be?

You can sell your business. Buyers will only be interested if the business is viable without you. If you are the business, then once you have gone there is nothing to buy, except possibly the brand name and whatever stock and equipment is left over, along with your customer list if it has any value. Within the business community there is a common prejudice against buying businesses that rely on the talent and drive of a single individual. Once you have considered your long-term options,

Exit strategy options

- You can simply quit. If you run a small business, or provide a service that is based on your individual talent, this could be your only realistic option. Unless you have built up a team of staff, your business cannot exist without your skills. On the upside, retirement from this sort of self-employment is relatively simple, as you are less likely to have premises or large numbers of staff to deal with. As long as you have invested wisely for your future, winding up your business should be painless.

- If your business can operate without your presence on a daily basis, you can hand over the day-to-day running to a business manager, or someone else in your family. You retain ownership and ultimate control, but leave most of the hard work to someone else. This can be an attractive option if you are the type that finds it easy to make the break from one way of life to another. However, it depends on having built up a reasonably extensive business, which has the turnover and infrastructure to support this sort of management arrangement.

rethink your future. Is your business going to provide you with just an income, or are you also looking at a growing asset? If that is the case, you need to create something that has real value that can outlast your existence within the business. This would typically include:

- Unique products.
- A superb brand.
- Exclusive distributor agreements with suppliers.
- Service agreements with customers.
- Historical profitable partnership agreements.

The long term

195

- A unique or patented service that you can replicate under licence.
- An effective management and organisational structure.
- Property, equipment or other items on the balance sheet.

The selling process

There is a healthy market for the buying and selling of businesses, but your success in it will depend on your business and its sector. Ideally, the decision to sell should be taken several years before the event. This will give you time to maximise your profitability over the period leading up to the sale. This is advisable as the value of businesses is most commonly calculated as a multiple of profits. Your accountant (or alternatively, a specialist business sales organisation) will give you best advice on the action to take.

PENSIONS AND INVESTMENTS

Let us return to thinking about your personal future. One area that is often overlooked by the self-employed is personal financial security. Many self-employed workers do not have a pension, which is a risky position to be in. When you start your business, especially if you start young, the need for a pension can seem remote, and besides, as far as you are concerned your business is going to make you so rich you will not need one.

For most self-employed people it does not quite work out that way, so it is a good idea to make some investment in your financial future, especially as the state pension seems to be in terminal decline.

As well as pensions, it is a good idea to use your money wisely. This is an area where a good accountant can earn his or her fee. If you make the most of ISA allowances and Capital Gains Tax and relief, you could invest substantial amounts of income tax-free. It may also be worth your while to consult an independent financial adviser about your personal assets and how best to manage them.

GROWING YOUR BUSINESS

So you have taken the plunge and are now the owner of a brand new business. Congratulations. The planning, preparation and launch of any business is hard work. Now that it is up and running, you can catch your breath. However, this is no time to stop. If you want your business to provide a long-term income, you need to think about growth. If it is to succeed, you will need to keep moving forward, standing still is not an option.

Successful growth does not necessarily mean that you have to evolve from a one-man band to a multinational conglomerate. The great thing about running your own business is that you have control over it and you can make it grow in the way that you want it to. You may enjoy being small. If so, you can manage it so that your business remains small. But that is not the same thing as standing still. If you do not move forward, competitors will overtake you and drain away your customers. Throughout this book we have stressed the importance of fulfilling the needs of your defined market. Markets rarely stand still, and it is important that you change your business to suit their evolving demands. This is an essential part of the growth process.

It is important that you end up running the sort of business that you want to. If one of your motivations for starting-up was that you wanted to take control of your life, you might find that owning a big business has precisely the opposite effect: the responsibility of running a complex organisation can erode your freedom just as much as living the life of a wage slave.

> **The great thing about running your own business is that you have control over it and you can make it grow in the way that you want it to.**

Alternatively you could find the confines of a small business too claustrophobic, and feel the need to put in place the processes for large-scale growth as soon as possible. The point is that planning the future of your business is vital. Success is hard enough to achieve as it is, but if you simply let it happen in an unplanned way, you risk returning to the dissatisfied state that may have led you to leave full-time employment in the first place.

So assuming you have achieved your first objective, starting and establishing your business, let us consider the options you have for managing your business's future. As you make decisions about

whether or not to develop your business, you are likely to fall into one of the following categories:

- **The 'Steady Eddie' self-employed individual.** Each year you do your business, keep your customers happy and meet their needs with the products and services you supply. You gain new customers through referrals, but you do not necessarily go out your way to find them yourself. You are good at your job and are rarely short of work. However, you also have a number of contacts that sub-contract jobs for you to complete on their behalf.

- **The contractor/project leader.** You are good at what you do but you prefer to work through others. This allows you more time to develop your business. Having proved that there is business to be done in your chosen marketplace, you use freelancers or sub-contractors to deliver the goods and ensure their work meets your high standards. You manage customer relationships and the finances; you establish a network of customers and suppliers that provides on-going opportunities. In time, you may recruit a small number of people, perhaps an administrator or a contract manager. This allows you to take on more projects and take holidays while still being paid.

- **The employer.** You have established a business model but need others to make it work. Having considered freelance, sub-contractors, agency staff and employees, you choose to recruit a core team that you can motivate, train and develop. You manage the business. Because of the overheads involved in employing staff, you keep a close eye on the finances, perhaps using a part-time bookkeeper. You stay close to your customers and place a high priority on business development. You develop systems and a staff structure to ensure your people work effectively and are rewarded for results. This includes staff to whom you delegate specific tasks and deputies who can manage the business in your absence.

- **The multi-site operator.** This category applies if your business is based on retailing from a physical shop. You are a classic organiser, nothing is left to chance in your business, whether it is the wording of an advertisement or the way in which your customer enquiries are handled. For every situation, you have a process that your team can follow. You now look for a second retail site, somewhere that ideally mirrors your first outlet or improves upon it. Consider its location carefully. Who is going to manage it? Will you need to oversee it? (If you do, make sure it is close enough so that you do not waste valuable time travelling.) It is difficult to expand without risk, so plan carefully to limit your exposure. Make sure that if the worst does happen, your core business will survive. Exploit your strengths, use all the knowledge you have built up from your successful operation to establish the foundation for the second. If the new site is close enough to your original, you can take advantage of shared promotions and advertising. Centralise your

administration, buying, and other key services to save on overheads. Once your second site is established and profitable, you have proved that your business can sustain expansion. Your next move may be to consider creating a franchise model.

- **The innovator.** You are good at identifying opportunities and driving change. Almost certainly you will be concentrated on a specific market, which over time can change, but taking a focused approach to customer needs is critical in this role. You understand your customers' needs in great depth, creating products and services they want, sometimes before they have even realised they need them. You lead the market and do everything you can to raise your profile. You develop your organisation by recruiting and developing people in key positions and give them the opportunity to grow. You generate an income through others. You can comfortably go on holiday in the knowledge that your business is increasing in value. Your unique products and services give you a competitive edge and, as a result, you make greater profits.

- **The acquisition expert.** You have a solid business, with high standards which provides consistent growth and profit. You build relationships with other organisations that also deliver products and services to the same market. When the time is right, you take advantage of opportunities to acquire other businesses that are closely aligned with your own market. These are always low-risk acquisitions, you are buying turnover, profit and established infrastructure. In addition you are looking at businesses that have failed to fulfill potential, but when partnered with your infrastructure, have the potential to accelerate without risk to your core business. You consistently take sound legal and financial advice and purchase at the right time. You delegate effectively, think strategically and let good quality people manage the day-to-day running of your businesses. Through your consistent strategy of acquisition, you strengthen your own financial position. The value of your companies allows you to borrow more funds to acquire others and your new size allows you to win major contracts, perhaps on an international basis. Your business is now exceptionally valuable and several large organisations are seeking to buy you out. Alternatively, you could 'go public', offering shares in your business to the general public via a listing on a small-cap stock exchange such as AIM (the Alternative Investment Market).

Useful addresses

ACCOUNTANT – TO FIND ONE

Association of Chartered Certified
Accountants
2 Central Quay
89 Hydepark Street
Glasgow G3 8BW
Tel: 0141 582 2000
www.acca.co.uk

Institute of Chartered Accountants
in England and Wales
PO Box 433
Moorgate Place
London EC2P 2BJ
Tel: 0207 920 8100
www.icaew.co.uk

Institute of Chartered Accountants
in Ireland
CA House, 83 Pembroke Road
Dublin 4
Republic of Ireland
Tel: (00 353) 1 637 7200
www.icai.ie

Institute of Chartered Accountants
of Scotland
CA House, 21 Haymarket Yards
Edinburgh EH12 5BH
Tel: 0131 347 0100
www.icas.org.uk

BUSINESS ADVICE – GOVERNMENT FUNDED

Business Link (England)
Tel: 0845 600 9 006
www.businesslink.gov.uk

Business Gateway (Scotland)
Tel: 0845 609 6611
www.bgateway.com

Highlands and Islands Enterprise
Cowan House
Inverness Retail and Business Park
Inverness IV2 7GF
Tel: 01463 234171
www.hie.co.uk

Business Eye/Llygad Busnes (Wales)
Tel: 08457 96 97 98
www.businesseye.org.uk

Invest Northern Ireland
www.investni.com

British Business Angels Association
The New City Court
20 St Thomas Street
London SE1 9RS
Tel: 0207 089 2305
www.bbaa.org.uk

The British Chambers of Commerce

65 Petty France
London SW1H 9EU
www.chamberonline.co.uk

The British Franchise Association (BFA)

Thames View
Newtown Road
Henley-on-Thames
Oxon RG9 1HG
Tel: 01491 578050
www.thebfa.org

British Insurance Brokers' Association

14 Bevis Marks
London EC3A 7NT
www.biba.org.uk

BSI Group

Tel: 020 8996 9001
www.standardswork.co.uk
Small business arm of the BSI Group
(British Standards Institute).

The Carbon Trust

8th Floor, 3 Clement's Inn
London WC2A 2AZ
Tel: 0800 085 2005
Helps business and the public sector
to cut carbon emissions.

Confederation of British Industry (CBI)

Centre Point
103 New Oxford Street
London WC1A 1DU
Tel: 0207 379 7400
www.cbi.org.uk
Lobbying organisation supporting
business interests in the UK.

The Department for Business, Enterprise and Regulatory Reform (DBERR)

1 Victoria Street
London SW1H 0ET
Tel: 020 7215 5000
www.dberr.gov.uk
www.sbs.gov.uk (Small Business Service)
redirects to DBERR's small business
pages.

Equality Direct

Tel: 0845 600 3444
www.equalitydirect.org.uk
Free advice for business owners and
managers on equality law.

The Environment Agency/ NetRegs

www.netregs.gov.uk
Advice for businesses on saving
resources and complying with
environmental regulations.

European Small Business Alliance

Rue Vautier 54
B-1050 Brussels
Belgium
Tel: +32 2 639 62 31
www.esba-europe.org
Independent organisation promoting interests of the self-employed throughout the EU.

The Factors and Discount Association (FDA)

Boston House, The Little Green
Richmond
Surrey TW9 1QE
020 8332 9955
www.thefda.org.uk
Professional association of debt factors in the UK.

The Federation of Small Businesses

Sir Frank Whittle Way
Blackpool Business Park
Blackpool FY4 2FE
Tel: 01253 336000
www.fsb.org.uk

Forum of Public Business

Ruskin Chambers
Drury Lane
Knutsford
Cheshire WA16 6HA
www.fpb.co.uk
Organisation offering membership services including practical help with running a small business.

Fredericks Foundation

Fredericks House
39 Guildford Road
Lightwater
Surrey GU18 5SA
Tel: 01276 472 722
www.fredericksfoundation.org
Advice and support for the financially disadvantaged, unemployed, single parents, ex-offenders and people with disabilities.

Growing your own Business

Venture Marketing Group
Carlton Plaza
111 Upper Richmond Road
London SW15 2TJ
Tel: 020 8394 5100
www.growingyourownbusiness.co.uk
Business advice conferences and networking opportunities.

HM Revenue and Customs

New Employer Helpline:
0845 6 070 143
NI Registration Helpline:
0845 915 7006
Self-Assessment Helpline:
0845 900 0444
Self-Employed Contact Centre:
0845 915 4655
Tax Credits Helpline:
0845 300 3900
www.hmrc.gov.uk
Local tax offices are not uniformly listed in telephone directories. You can find yours by visiting www.hmrc.gov.uk/local/individuals/

The Health and Safety Executive

Rose Court, 2 Southwark Bridge
London SE1 9HS
Tel: 0845 345 055
www.hse.gov.uk

The Institute of Business Consulting

Management House
Cottingham Road
Corby
Northants NN17 1TT
www.ibconsulting.org.uk
Tel: 01536 207307

The Institute of Direct Marketing

1 Park Road
Teddington
Middlesex TW11 0AR
Tel: 020 8614 0277
www.theidm.co.uk
Promotes DM best practice and provides global DM services and consultancy.

Institute of Directors (IoD)

116 Pall Mall
London SW1Y 5ED
Tel: 020 7839 1233
www.iod.com
Global, lobbying and business support organisation representing directors from the largest public companies to the smallest private firms.

The Learning and Skills Council

Cheylesmore House
Quinton Road
Coventry CV1 2WT
Tel: 0845 019 4170
www.lsc.gov.uk

Leonard Cheshire Ready to Start

Tel: 08456 717173
www.readytostart.org.uk
Charity that offers a network of financial experts, business entrepreneurs, disability groups and 'personal buddies from Barclays Bank' to support people with disabilities who wish to start in business.

Make Your Mark

6 Mercer Street
Covent Garden
London WC2H 9QA
Tel: 020 7497 4030
www.starttalkingideas.org
National campaign to create an enterprise culture among young people in the UK.

National Federation of Enterprise Agencies

12 Stephenson Court
Fraser Road
Priory Business Park
Bedford MK44 3WJ
Tel: 01234 831623
www.nfea.com
Network of independent, not for profit, Local Enterprise Agencies committed 203to the needs of start-ups, small and growing businesses.

PRIME

Astral House
1268 London Rd
London SW16 4ER
Tel: 0800 783 1904
www.primeinitiative.org.uk
A registered charity linked to Age Concern England, PRIME helps people over the age of 50 set up in business.

The Prince's Trust (UK-wide)

18 Park Square East
London NW1 4LH
Tel: 0800 842 842
www.princes-trust.org.uk

Prince's Scottish Youth Business Trust (Scotland)

15 Exchange Place
Glasgow G1 3AN
Tel: 0141 248 4999
www.psybt.org.uk

Shell LiveWire

Unit 15 Design Works
William Street
Felling
Gateshead NE10 0JP
Tel: 0191 423 6229
www.shell-livewire.com
A worldwide organisation for young entrepreneurs aged 16-30.

The Small Business Bureau Limited

Curzon House
Church Road
Windlesham
Surrey GU20 6BH
Tel: 01276 452010/452020
www.smallbusinessbureau.co.uk
Independent organisation promoting business interests in the UK. It is the parent organisation behind Women into Business.

The Small Firms Enterprise Development Initiative (SFEDI)

PO Box 159
Newton Aycliffe
DL5 6WE
www.sfedi.co.uk
A body started by the Department of Trade and Industry. Trains and certifies business advisers and offers a range of support services to small businesses.

Start your own Business

PO Box Eastleigh
SO50 0AA
Tel: 023 8074 0400
www.syob.co.uk
Free local guide providing useful local information to anyone thinking of setting up on their own in each area of the UK.

SOLICITOR – TO FIND ONE

The Law Society (England and Wales)
Tel: 0870 606 2555
www.lawsociety.org.uk

The Law Society of Northern Ireland
40 Linenhall Street
Belfast BT2 8BA
Tel: 028 9023 1614
www.lawsoc-ni.org

The Law Society of Scotland
26 Drumsheugh Gardens
Edinburgh EH3 7YR
Tel: 0131 226 7411
www.lawscot.org.uk

Technology Means Business

c/o IT Forum Foundation Ltd
Winkworth House
83 St Judes Road
Englefield Green
Surrey TW20 0DF
Tel: 01784 473005
www.technologymeansbusiness.org.uk
Accrediting body for consultants and advisers offering information and communications technology support to small businesses.

UK Business Incubation

Faraday Wharf
Aston Science Park
Holt Street
Birmingham B7 4BB
Tel: 0121 250 3538
www.ukbi.co.uk

UK Trade & Investment

Tay House
300 Bath Street
Glasgow G2 4DX
0207 215 8000
www.uktradeinvest.gov.uk
Government body designed to help UK businesses trade overseas. You can find you local office via the website.

UK Web Design Association (UKWDA)

www.ukwda.org
Accredits web design providers in the UK and offers site visitors a search facility for finding UKWDA-affiliated web design companies.

Young Enterprise UK

Peterley House
Peterley Road
Oxford OX4 2TZ
Tel: 01865 776845
Business education charity inspiring and supporting young people in enterprise.

Useful websites

BUSINESS ADVICE AND RESOURCES

www.adviceguide.org.uk Citizens Advice Bureau's guide to self-employment.

www.axa4business.co.uk Advice on running a small business, plus resources and a free consultancy service from one of the world's largest insurance companies, AXA.

www.bcentral.co.uk Software giant Microsoft's contribution to the world of small business advice.

www.businessbricks.co.uk One of the UK's most popular small business newsletters and blogs.

www.businessclub365.com Advice, guidance and buying power for small business and startups.

www.everywoman.co.uk Business resource for female entrepreneurs and women business owners.

www.j4b.co.uk Allows users to search a comprehensive listing of UK business grants.

www.kompass.co.uk A searchable directory of over 2 million businesses worldwide. Useful for finding partners and clients, and identifying competitors.

www.smallbusiness.co.uk A comprehensive web portal offering advice on all aspects of starting and running a small business.

www.smallbusinessadvice.org.uk Useful links and articles, plus downloadable templates for cashflow, P&L forecasts and business plans.

www.ukbusinessforums.co.uk A lively online forum for business discussion and advice.

MAJOR OUTSOURCING PROVIDERS

www.elance.com
www.freelancers.net
www.freelancersintheuk.co.uk
www.guru.com
www.rentacoder.com

WEB/ECOMMERCE/SEO ADVICE AND ASSISTANCE

www.apple.com/uk UK homepage for Apple computers, featuring downloads and updates for Mac users.

www.google.com/adsense Google's pay-per-click (PPC) advertising hosting service.

www.google.com/adwords The same as Adsense, but for advertisers.

www.seochat.com Articles, advice and forums on all aspects of search engine optimisation.

www.sitepoint.net/forums Discussion on search engine optimisation, web design and ecommerce.

www.w3.org The World Wide Web Consortium. A comprehensive guide to web standards. The site also includes exhaustive glossaries and tutorials for would-be web developers.

www.webmonkey.com Guides to basic web technologies such as HTML, CSS and JavaScript.

www.webdesignforbusiness.org A detailed overview of web design, offering advice and guidance. Developed by the Design Council (www.designcouncil.org.uk)

publisher.yahoo.com Pay-per-click (PPC) ad network from search engine Yahoo!

SOFTWARE, ADVICE AND ASSISTANCE

www.basecamphq.com Web-based document sharing and project management.

www.google.com/docs Wordprocessing and spreadsheet software. Multiple users can access a single account, allowing project collaboration. Files can be compatible with Microsoft Word and Excel.

www.kashflow.co.uk Straightforward accounting software.

www.mrexcel.com Online forum dedicated to solving problems with Microsoft's Excel spreadsheet software.

www.openoffice.org Open source suite of office and business software.

office.microsoft.com Microsoft's own help resource for its Office suite of applications.

www.paypal.co.uk Financial transaction handling.

www.sage.co.uk Accounting software and business advice.

www.sourceforge.net Comprehensive listing of open source software.

www.taxcalc.com Self-assessment software designed with the UK market in mind.

www.turbocashuk.com Open source accounting software aimed at UK users.

207

Glossary

3G The high-speed 'third generation' of mobile phone data networks.

Address book A function of most email applications that allows you to store, organise and retrieve email addresses.

Advertising The part of marketing that deals with directly persuading members of your target market to buy your product or service.

Affiliate marketing Using the internet to promote someone else's products without having to buy or hold any stock yourself. Everything remains with the manufacturer or main dealer, who handles the payment process and shipping and pays you a commission for every sale you make.

Application A piece of computer software that allows you perform a specific task, such as word-processing. In casual conversation it's often used interchangeably with 'program'.

Bandwidth The amount of data you are allowed to download over your internet connection in a given time, usually a month.

Bangtail A detachable extension, with a perforated edge, found on the back of an envelope. It is normally used to contain marketing information or an order form, such as a reply-paid slip.

Bluetooth A radio technology that allows mobile phones, computers and other electronic devices to exchange information.

Brand The reputation and character of your business, and product, or both, in the eyes of your target market.

Brand values The qualities you want your target market to associate with your brand. Brand values may include value, reliability, friendliness, speed of service and many other characteristics. Most businesses concentrate on developing three or four key brand values.

Business angel A private investor who brings both expertise and equity finance to start-ups.

Cashflow forecast An assessment of how cash is likely to flow throw your business. This is explained in greater detail in Chapter 5.

Companies House The London-based government organisation that registers, monitors and keeps records of all UK companies. All limited companies are registered with Companies House, sole traders are not.

Credit reference agency An agency such as Experian, Equifax and Callcredit, which shares information with banks and lending agencies on an individual's credit history. Individuals have a legal right to access the data that is held on them.

Creditors The people and businesses that your business owes money to.

CRM products Customer Relationship Management software packages which typically allow you to make notes while you are on the phone, book appointments, set tasks and reminders and, most important of all, have this information readily available next time the customer calls. You can also share CRM data automatically with associates or employees.

Demographics A method of defining target markets and groups of people in terms of age, income, location, personal interests and other factors. You can use this information to identify a 'target demographic' for your business.

Debtors The people and businesses that owe money to your business.

Domain name The internet address of your website. It is also sometimes referred to as a URL (short for 'Uniform Resource Locator').

Ecommerce The buying and selling of products and services using the internet to manage the whole sales process.

eBay A trading website, www.ebay.com, which allows people all over the world to buy and sell new and used items to one another.

Equity finance The money you put into a business yourself, or the money that you persuade an investor or business partner to contribute in exchange for a share of the profits.

Gatefold A foldout, especially one that opens to double the page size, used most frequently in marketing leaflets.

Incubator An investment business or organisation that supports start-ups through equity finance, business advice and mentoring and physical support, such as the provision of a serviced office.

IPO Initial Public Offering, where a business presents itself to a stock market prior to flotation. It allows potential investors to learn about the business, and conversely, allows a business to gauge the level of interest among potential investors.

Limited Liability Partnership (LLP) A business structure that operates under the limited liability of an ordinary limited company while retaining the structure of a partnership.

List broker An agency that retains data on thousands of individuals and businesses. A list broker will ask you about your target market and compile a list of addresses, or telephone numbers, or both, of potential customers (sometimes called 'prospects').

Margin The profit you make on a product or service, considered as the proportion of the selling price that isn't eaten up by expenses.

Marketing The process of learning about your target market and communicating with it. Marketing also includes some elements of product development and presentation.

Marketing materials The print or digital materials you produce to support your marketing effort. This includes your website and printed items like brochures and flyers. They are also sometimes referred to as 'marketing collateral'.

Niche marketing Refining your product offer and marketing approach so they appeal to a very narrow, specific group of potential customers, a 'niche'. Aiming at a niche means you can specialise and create an offer more likely to appeal to your customers.

NICO National Insurance Contributions Office, the part of HM Revenue & Customs that deals with the collection and recording of National Insurance contributions.

Offer The combination of a product and its price when presented to a target market.

Open source software Mainly free software programs with licences that allow users to run them for any purpose.

They are also open to modification or development, and allow users to redistribute copies of either the original or the modified program without having to pay royalties to previous developers.

P45 The document you receive from your former employer to confirm you have ceased to work for that company.

Paper stock The type of card or paper. This may be coated or uncoated, matt or glossy and of a greater or lesser degree of quality. Individual stocks may also be produced in different weights.

PAYE An acronym for Pay As You Earn, the HMRC system for collecting tax from full-time employees of a business or an organisation.

Payment gateway A third party web-based business such as PayPal that takes payments on your behalf, saving you the hassle of getting a credit card merchant account with a bank.

Pitch A pitch is any presentation where you try to sell your business idea. An example could be when you are presenting a business plan to a bank manager in a bid to raise capital to start your business.

POS An acronym standing for Point of Sale. This is where customers are presented with marketing materials at the point where they buy your product. This may be a flyer positioned next to the till in a shop, or a marketing freebie given to the customer along with the product or service they purchase.

Profit and loss forecast Similar to a cashflow forecast, but based on actual profits and losses rather than simple cash payments.

Public-facing A business that works with the public on a daily basis. Includes shops, service and repair businesses and several other categories.

Search engine Websites such as Google, Yahoo! and MSN that search the internet for the words or terms requested by the user.

Search engine optimisation The use of techniques, both free and paid-for, to drive your website to the top of the list that a search engine produces after completing a search.

Secondary drive A spare hard disk drive that can be attached to your computer via USB or FireWire cables and used as backup storage.

Self-certification mortgage Mortgages for the self-employed who cannot produce two of three years' worth of accounts backed by an accountant. These tend to demand payment at a higher rate to minimise risk, although the market is becoming more competitive and deals are improving.

SERPS An acronym standing for search engine results pages. This is the list of websites and webpages that your search engine displays after having completed a search for you.

Small-cap stock exchange A stock exchange with a smaller market capitalisation than would be permissible for a larger market, such as the London Stock Exchange.

SME Small to medium-sized enterprise, typically numbering 1-250 employees.

SoHo An acronym standing for small office – home office and is used as an umbrella term for all types of home workers and their home-based offices.

Spam Unwanted, unsolicited email from people you do not know, usually offering to sell you things you do not want.

Start-up finance The money you need to get your business off the ground.

Strapline A secondary sentence or slogan that is attached to a brand, logo or company name. Ideally, it is an easy to remember phrase that adds value to the core product or service and strengthens brand awareness.

Target market The group of consumers or businesses who have a need or a desire for your product, as well as the means and willingness to pay for it. A business may have just one target market or several.

Tax year A year that runs from 6 April to the following 5 April. It is the period over which your income is assessed for tax. You must complete one tax return for each tax year.

211

Trojan Horse Also known just as a Trojan, this is a destructive program that masquerades as a benign application. Unlike viruses, it doesn't replicate itself.

Venture capitalist These are investors who tend to be a bigger, brasher version of business angels and incubators. They provide (often very large) chunks of capital for both start-ups and businesses that require additional investment to grow. In return for their investment, they expect equity (normally in the form of shares) and often want a say in the running of the business. This is typically with a presence on the board of directors, but can also include providing business advice, skills, contacts and mentoring.

Web-based email An email application that is based on a website rather than a standalone email application. It allows you to check your email from any internet-connected computer in the world.

WEP Short for Wired Equivalent Privacy, WEP is designed to provide the same level of security as that of a wired local area network. In practice it is not normally as secure as standard wired networks as these tend to also have physical security such as walls and ceilings.

Wireless hub A radio base station that allows nearby computers (usually within 100m) to access the internet wirelessly.

Worm A program that replicates itself over a computer network and usually performs malicious actions.

Index

Index

Which? is the leading independent consumer champion in the UK.
A not-for-profit organisation, we exist to make individuals as powerful as the organisations they deal with in everyday life. The next few pages give you a taster of our many products and services. For more information, log onto www.which.co.uk or call 0800 252 100.

Which? magazine

Which? is, quite simply, the most trusted magazine in the UK. It takes the stress out of your buying decisions by offering independent, thoroughly researched advice on consumer goods and services from cars to current accounts via coffee makers. Its Best Buy recommendations are the gold standards in making sound and safe purchases across the nation. Which? has been making things happen for all consumers since 1957 – and you can join us by subscribing at www.which.co.uk or calling 0800 252 100 and quoting 'Which'.

Which? online

www.which.co.uk gives you access to all Which? content online. Updated daily, you can read hundreds of product reports and Best Buy recommendations, keep up to date with Which? campaigns, compare products, use our financial planning tools and interactive car-buying guide. You can also access all the reviews from the *The Which? Good Food Guide*, ask an expert in our interactive forums, register for e-mail updates and browse our online shop – so what are you waiting for? www.which.co.uk.

Which? Legal Service

The Which? Legal Service offers immediate access to first-class legal advice at unrivalled value. One low-cost annual subscription allows members to enjoy unlimited legal advice by telephone on a wide variety of legal topics, including consumer law (problems with goods and services), employment law, holiday problems, neighbour disputes and parking/speeding/clamping issues. Our qualified lawyers help members reach the best outcome in a user-friendly way, guiding them through each stage on a step-by-step basis. Call 0800 252 100 for more information or visit www.which.co.uk.

Which? Books

Other books in this series

The Pension Handbook
By Jonquil Lowe
ISBN: 978 1 84490 025 1
Price £10.99

A definitive guide to sorting out your pension, whether you're deliberating over SERPs/S2Ps, organising a personal pension or moving schemes. Cutting through confusion and dispelling apathy, Jonquil Lowe provides up-to-date advice on how to maximise your savings and provide for the future.

Giving and Inheriting
By Jonquil Lowe
ISBN: 978 1 84490 032 9
Price £10.99

Inheritance tax (IHT) is becoming a major worry for more and more people. Rising house prices have pushed up the value of typical estates to a level where they are liable to be taxed at 40% on everything over £285,000. *Giving and Inheriting* is an essential guide to estate planning and tax liability, offering up-to-the–minute advice from an acknowledged financial expert, this book will help people reduce the tax bill faced by their heirs and allow many to avoid IHT altogether.

Wills and Probate
By Paul Elmhirst
ISBN: 978 1 84490 033 6
Price £10.99

Wills and Probate provides clear, easy-to-follow guidance on the main provisions to make in a will and the factors you should consider when drafting these. The second part of the book provides step-by-step guidance on probate, making the process as straightforward and trouble-free as possible. By being aware of key changes and revisions and avoiding the problems and pitfalls, you can limit delays, avoid disputes and save tax.

Which? Books

Which? Books

Other books in this series

Buy, Sell and Move House
By Kate Faulkner
ISBN: 978 1 84490 043 5
Price £10.99

A complete, no-nonsense guide to negotiating the property maze and making your move as painless as possible. From dealing with estate agents to chasing solicitors, working out the true cost of your move to understanding Home Information Packs, this guide tells you how to keep things on track and avoid painful sticking points.

Renting and Letting
By Kate Faulkner
ISBN: 978 1 84490 029 9
Price £10.99

A practical guide for landlords, tenants, and anybody considering the buy-to-let market. Covering all the legal and financial matters, including tax, record-keeping and mortgages, as well as disputes, deposits and security, this book provides comprehensive advice for anybody involved in renting property.

Buying Property Abroad
By Jeremy Davies
ISBN: 978 1 84490 024 4
Price £10.99

A complete guide to the legal, financial and practical aspects of buying property abroad. This book provides down-to-earth advice on how the buying process differs from the UK, and how to negotiate contracts, commission surveys, and employ lawyers and architects. Practical tips on currency deals and taxes – and how to command the best rent – all ensure you can buy abroad with total peace of mind.

Which? Books

Which? Books provide impartial, expert advice on everyday matters from finance to law, property to major life events. We also publish the country's most trusted restaurant guide, *The Which? Good Food Guide*. To find out more about Which? Books, log on to www.which.co.uk or call 01903 828557.

" Which? tackles the issues that really matter to consumers and gives you the advice and active support you need to buy the right products. **"**